This book is one of its kind in India. Rodney and Ashwin have done a great job in writing on such a unique topic. I highly recommend this book.

—**Garry Singh**, *President, IIRIS Pvt Ltd*

The book is extremely informative and gives a deep insight into cyberattacks and data breaches, which can cause irreparable loss to a corporate organisation. A must-read for in-house counsels to prepare them to effectively counter such threats.

—**Siddhartha Pandit**, *Head of the Legal Department, Havells India Pvt Ltd*

Cyber crisis management is a unique topic on which many business books are not available. I strongly recommend this book written by Rodney and Ashwin. It is a must-read.

—**Gautam Vohra**, *General Counsel, Hike Messenger*

Cyber Crisis Management

Cyber Crisis Management

Overcoming the Challenges in Cyberspace

Rodney D. Ryder

Ashwin Madhavan

BLOOMSBURY

NEW DELHI • LONDON • OXFORD • NEW YORK • SYDNEY

BLOOMSBURY INDIA
Bloomsbury Publishing India Pvt. Ltd
Second Floor, LSC Building No. 4, DDA Complex, Pocket C – 6 & 7,
Vasant Kunj New Delhi 110070

BLOOMSBURY, BLOOMSBURY INDIA and the Diana logo are trademarks of Bloomsbury Publishing Plc

First published in India 2019
This edition published in 2019

ISBN: TPB: 978-93-89165-50-0; eBook: 978-93-89165-52-4

2 4 6 8 10 9 7 5 3 1

Typeset in Manipal Digital
Printed and bound in India by Replika Press Pvt. Ltd.

To Rebecca, Mark and Gunjan
—Rodney D. Ryder

To Bo, Mom, Dad and Naani
—Ashwin Madhavan

CONTENTS

PREFACE

It all began with a thought on cyber security and cyber management in the fall of 2017. I was vacationing in Obersalzberg, a small German town, very close to the country's border with Austria. My genuine excitement to write on this subject made me call my close friend and business partner—Rodney D. Ryder. Rodney is known to be an authority on this subject and it was natural for me to have called him. I was standing on one leg (literally!) while making this call and to my great happiness, Rodney agreed.

Our first task was to prepare an outline that would give the book a non-legal perspective. Our idea was to bring about a business-friendly, easy-to-understand book on this vital issue that is prevalent today and will remain so as long as computers exist on this planet.

With the outline and the synopsis ready, it was time for us to take upon ourselves the arduous task of finding a good publisher. After facing a couple of rejections, which was disappointing, we finally got the confirmation from one of the best in the publishing world—Bloomsbury. People from all walks of life, old and young, including crazy Harry Potter fans, will have come across books published by Bloomsbury, and both of us felt elated when the folks from Bloomsbury agreed to our proposal.

Then came the difficult task of putting our ideas on paper and getting into the grind of writing this manuscript, which, in our humble opinion, has not been attempted in India. Our mutual lifelong love for business strategy and our interest in the military history of the Second World War helped us in writing the chapters. During our discussion, Rodney envisioned that he wanted us to write a book that would not only be read by the CEOs and the CTOs of the organisation, but also by business managers, who need to develop skills vis-à-vis cyber crisis management in the digital age—an age which is becoming even more digital and vulnerable. The book, he suggested, should be a primer on the next corporate challenge of how to handle cyber incidences, of how to develop tactics to secure an organisation from cyberattacks, and on the relationship between cyber security and new technologies such as Artificial Intelligence and Cloud Computing.

Today, on my birthday, when we have finally finished writing this book after several painstaking reviews along with our group of researchers, I genuinely hope that you, the reader, find this an interesting read.

Ashwin Madhavan
24 April 2019

ACKNOWLEDGEMENTS

Any book written by an author is a collaborative effort of like-minded individuals with the sole aim to write good content that is easy to understand and comprehend. Over the last many months, we have been fortunate to get valuable inputs, suggestions and foundational research from across the length and breadth of India.

Among the many young, old and smart people that we have interacted with in the past 24 months, who gave their time generously and provided their wisdom to this effort, we wish to thank (in alphabetical order):

Debarghya Mitra, Garima Punjabi, Manisha Gupta, Mobina Ali, Prakarsh Seth, Ritu Chopra, Sattik Rout and Sohini Mukherjee.

In addition to those mentioned earlier, we wish to thank Vidisha Joshi, who helped us during the first drafts of the book and aided us in fishing through the voluminous content; she managed the research team 'remotely' (yes, you read that correctly!) from Bengaluru and her hometown of Korba, Chhattisgarh.

We also cannot thank enough the members of the team at Bloomsbury for standing by us for the past two years. Praveen Tiwari, Nitin Valecha and Shreya Chakraborti have helped us thoroughly during the final months of writing the book.

We come now to the one individual without whose help this book would have gone nowhere. Debasmita Haldar's extraordinary contribution to this book in the form of research and putting things in the right perspective was truly amazing. This book would not have been possible without her. It is generally said that authors burn the midnight oil to produce good work; but in our case, we can safely mention that Debasmita stood by us like a rock during the entire process of writing this book.

Finally, we want to thank our immediate families for their support during our long two-year effort to complete this book.

1

CYBER MANAGEMENT AND CYBER SECURITY

In the past 15 years, the Internet has transformed our lives to a great extent. In fact, it has become an essential part of our daily lives. However, with an increase in technological advancements in the area of the Internet, the amount of illicit activities relating to cyberspace has multiplied as well. Cyber-security breaches, such as data breaches and various other cybercrimes, have plagued the Internet since the beginning of the second decade of the 21st century.

A Scary Situation!

Top management officials are clueless about how to handle cyberattacks.

The rise in the number of crimes related to the Internet is no longer limited to social media. It also involves data theft and cyberattacks in various organisations. Cyberattacks against organisations have become such a nightmare for business owners and data security experts, that many a time, the organisation experiences a cyberattack and its top management may never know the harm such attacks can cause. Isn't this scary? Many top management officials are clueless about how to handle cyberattacks, which in the end, leads to, not only loss of reputation of the organisation, but also a huge loss in terms of money.

How to Survive?

In order to survive a fatal cyberattack or data theft, organisations need to be careful and keep themselves equipped with the state-of-the-art cyber-security tools. They should be able to deftly manage a cyber-security problem through proper planning and making use of their human resources to deal with it.

> *Cyberattacks and cyber breaches undoubtedly create huge risks and can be a death sentence for organisations if not properly managed.*

We, through this book, have tried our best to explain what you, as a reader, need to know and understand about cyber crisis management. In our opinion, cyberattacks and cyber breaches undoubtedly create huge risks and can be a death sentence to organisations if not properly managed. The only way to survive an onslaught of cyberattacks is to be prepared in advance with proper tools and proper planning.

But, before getting into the nitty-gritty of cyber crisis management, let us help you understand the meaning of the term—cyber security.

What Is Cyber Security?

Cyber security, as the word suggests, means protecting your vital computer assets (be it hardware or software) from potential misuse. In other words, cyber security can be defined as a practice of insuring the integrity and confidentiality of information and protecting its availability. It represents the ability to defend or protect against and recover from mishaps like hard-drive failures or power outages, cybercrimes and data theft. It basically focuses on protecting the computers, the network and a huge amount of data that can lead to irreparable damages because of being accessed unlawfully or without authorisation.

Not an Easy Task!

Management of cyber security is not an easy task anymore, as it involves a myriad of devices, increased data networks and eventually gives rise to opportunities of exploitation too.

> *Cyber security can be defined as a practice of insuring the integrity and confidentiality of information and protecting its availability.*

The next question that comes to our minds is the need to secure our cyberspace. We have somewhat explained this question on the first page, but would like to explain it a little more.

Why Do We Need to Secure Our Cyberspace?

In today's world, when access to Internet is just a click away, our lives revolve around it. We just can't stop expressing our indefinite love for the Internet and usually forget that the Internet is a package of both positives and negatives. While the Internet is awesome and fascinating to almost everyone who has come in contact with it, it is needless to mention that the Internet is not as secure as it may seem.

No statistics or records are enough to define the large number of cyberattacks that organisations and users in general are facing every day.

Did You Know?

The number of cyber-security attacks is increasing every year. From a total cost of $445 billion in 2014, the cost of cybercrime-related incidents reached up to $600 billion in 2017 amounting to 0.8% of the world's GDP.

Source: 'The Economic Impact of Cybercrime—No Slowing Down'. https://www.mcafee.com/enterprise/en-us/assets/reports/restricted/rp-economic-impact-cybercrime.pdf?utm_source=Press&utm_campaign=bb9303ae70-EMAIL_CAMPAIGN_2018_02_21&utm_medium=email

Is Cybercrime a Global Economic Problem?

A cyberattack stains the goodwill of an organisation.

McAfee, the world's leading independent cyber-security expert, through its report titled *The Economic Impact of Cybercrime—No Slowing Down* (February 2018), has stated that cybercrime ranks third, behind corruption and narcotics, as a global economic problem.

Numerous companies including government organisations have frequently been victims of cyberattacks and this hasn't been an easy phase for anyone. Organisations that are involved in keeping personal data safe for their clients are often targeted for cyberattacks, which not only causes a loss of millions of dollars every year, but also stains the goodwill of the organisation that witnesses such an incident.

The need for cyber security is not necessarily because cyberattacks are increasing in number day by day, but it is because the degree of cyberattacks is destructive. To put it straight, no one has easily escaped from its paws, if once caught.

Let us now discuss the various types of cyberattacks that organisations experience across the world.

Types of Cyber-security Attacks ('We Are Being Attacked!')

Most common types of cyber-security attacks include:

- Malware
- Phishing
- SQL injection
- Denial of Service (DoS)
- Cross-site Scripting (XSS)

To put it straight, no one has escaped from the jaws of a cyberattack.

Malware

What is malware?

Malware is the short form of *malicious software*, which means software that can be used to compromise a computer's function, its data and eventually cause severe harm to the host computer.

Types of malware are:

- Adware
- Bots
- Bugs
- Spyware
- Rootkit
- Ransomware
- Virus
- Worm
- Trojan Horse

Did You Know?

Malware can get into your system via social networking sites. It is advised not to click on any random link as they often lead to malware intrusion. Social network is the most preferred place for hackers as most of the links that are connected to malware attacks are shared by mutual contacts which people click on without applying any second thought.

Source: 'Internet Security 101: Six Ways Hackers Can Attack You and How to Stay Safe'. https://economictimes.indiatimes.com/tech/internet/internet-security-101-six-ways-hackers-can-attack-you-and-how-to-stay-safe/articleshow/61342742.cms?from=mdr

Malware symptoms

Just as a human being exhibits certain symptoms such as high fever, sore throat and running nose when he/she is infected with common cold virus/bacteria, similarly, a computer system of an individual user or an organisation exhibits the following symptoms, when it is infected with malware:

- Increased CPU usage
- Slow web browser or computer speed
- Freezing or crashing
- Modified or deleted files
- Strange computer behaviour and errors
- Exchange of strange emails without the user's knowledge

How to protect your device from a malware attack?

An organisation/user can become a victim of a hazardous malware attack any time if he/she doesn't take any preventive step to stop such a cyberattack. An organisation/user can follow certain preventive steps, as stated in the following box, to protect their Information Technology (IT) systems from any malware attacks:

Preventive Steps

- *Install an anti-malware and firewall software:* Always make sure that you/your organisation chooses a software, which provides you with tools for detecting, quarantining and removing malware irrespective of their types.

- *Update your systems*: A user should always make sure that his/her device is always equipped with an up-to-date operating system; the operating system should always be updated with possible vulnerability patches to make sure that no attacker exploits your device.

- *Download only from safe and secure sources*: Never download files or programs from any unauthorised source; if you do so, more are the chances that you become the victim of a hazardous malware attack.

Did You Know?

Around 2,30,000 new malware samples are produced every day—and this is predicted to only keep growing.

Source: '24 Cybersecurity Statistics that Matter in 2019'. https://preyproject.com/blog/en/24-cybersecurity-statistics-that-matter-in-2019/

Phishing

What is a phishing attack?

Phishing is a type of a cyberattack where an email or a malicious website is used to get hold of personal or confidential data of individuals or organisations. The major goal of a phishing attack is to dupe the targeted individual or organisation to such an extent that they would voluntarily or inadvertently provide sensitive information to the attacker.

Types of phishing attacks

The most common types of phishing attacks are:

- Deceptive phishing
- Spear phishing
- CEO fraud
- Pharming
- Dropbox phishing
- Google Docs phishing

What is deceptive phishing?

Deceptive phishing is the most common phishing attack. In such phishing attacks, the attacker impersonates a legitimate organisation and attempts to steal the personal information of the targeted individual.

What is spear phishing?

This kind of phishing attack is a little more sophisticated and follows a carefully thought-out plan. In spear phishing scams, attackers customise their emails, with the target's name, designation, phone number and other important professional information, which compels the recipient of the email to believe that he/she has a connection with the sender of the email.

Did You Know?

Spear phishing is especially commonplace on social media sites like LinkedIn where attackers can use multiple sources of information to craft a targeted attack email.

Source: 'Review of Phishing Attacks and Anti Phishing Tools'. http://www.ijircce.com/upload/2017/september/49_Final_Paper%20_16_.pdf

What is CEO fraud?

This kind of a phishing attack targets senior-level executives of the company. In such cases, the fraudster impersonates the email ID of the CEO of the targeted organisation and starts sending emails authorising financial transactions directed to a bank account associated with the fraudster himself.

What is pharming?

Pharming is a kind of an attack that has its roots in the Domain Name System or DNS. In this, the fraudster penetrates the DNS of the target company's website. The fraudster targets the DNS server and then tampers with the IP address of the website with an alphabetical website name, thereby redirecting legitimate users of that particular website to a malicious website that the fraudster has created, even if the users have entered the correct website name.

What are Dropbox phishing and Google Docs phishing?

With Dropbox and Google Docs gaining popularity, fraudsters use fake Dropbox accounts and Google Docs to lure people into using them.

> **Did You Know?**
>
> Businesses are increasingly faced with new 'fake login' phishing pages, mostly mimicking Microsoft, Office 365 and One Drive sites and landing pages.
>
> Source: 'Rapid7 Quarterly Threat Report'. https://content.rapid7.com/c/rapid7-threat-report-1?x=6MSrAi

How to identify phishing attacks?

Have you received any email stating that you have won a lottery of $50,000? But, you have never ever enrolled for such a lottery. This is what is a phishing attack. Such emails ask for your personal account details and promise a quick way to win a lot of money. If you're someone who desperately needs money, then you might be an easy target of a phishing attack.

> *Have you received any email stating that you have won a lottery of $50,000? But you have never ever enrolled for such lottery. This is a phishing attack!*

Whenever you receive any email promising you a huge sum of money or a mail stating a state of urgency or an email asking for your account details, make sure that the email comes from an authorised organisation or entity. In case of doubt, call up and enquire, but never ever click on any links provided to you in that email or provide confidential information without cross-checking the authenticity of the sender.

How to protect your device from a phishing attack?

A phishing attack can be severe and may amount to a huge loss. The only way to protect your device and data from becoming the target of a phishing attack is to be alert and to follow some simple rules such as:

- Beware of emails or pop-up links which seek your personal data; never click on unauthorised links.
- Secure your computer with a firewall, spam filters, antivirus and anti-spyware software.
- In case of confusion or doubt regarding such emails, call or confirm from an authorised authority.

SQL injection

What is an SQL injection attack?

SQL (Standardised Query Language) Injection attack is a cyberattack which is executed by malicious SQL statements. These malicious statements are executed by the attackers to manipulate the user's data or the functioning of a website. These SQL injection attacks can provide the attacker with unauthorised access to the customer's data by which they can either alter data or totally wipe it out from the system. At times, attackers can use an SQL injection attack to gain authority as an administrator of a website. They can alter passwords and completely wipe out the authorised administrator's role.

How to prevent an SQL injection attack?

To protect your website or webpage from an SQL injection attack, you can use the Website Application Firewall (WAF) security service which protects your website from any data theft or alteration. Basically, WAFs clear out your codes and files, if it suspects any kind of malware or possibility of an SQL injection attack.

Denial of Service (DoS)

What is a Denial of Service (DoS) attack?

A cyberattack wherein the primary aim of attackers or hackers is to prevent legitimate users from accessing the service or, in other words, deny service to legitimate users, either by flooding or crashing of services, is termed as a Denial of Service or a DoS attack. The attacker floods the target network or server with excessive messages containing authentication requests, but invalid return addresses. When the server attempts to send back authentication approval, it is unable to locate such addresses (since they are invalid) and ends up waiting before closing the connection. Just as the server has closed the connection, the attacker sends even more authentication messages containing invalid return addresses. The server authenticates, fails to locate the returning addresses, waits and the loop continues. The resultant effect is that the network/server is kept busy, and deprives intended users of its services.

Types of DoS attacks

Various types of DoS attacks are:

- Bandwidth attack

- Service request flood
- SYN flooding attack
- ICMP flood attack
- Peer-to-peer attack
- Permanent DoS attack
- Application level flood attack

How to identify a DoS attack?

Whenever your device is under the threat of a DoS attack, your device will either freeze completely for a while or the server might crash or your device will start working slowly. It might show an Error 503 (Service Unavailable) to the users.

How to prevent a DoS attack?

To prevent any DoS attack, you should install dotDefender web application firewall; it defends and inspects your http traffic against any attack that might stop the normal functioning of your system.

Cross-site scripting (XSS)

What is a cross-site scripting (XSS) attack?

Cross-site scripting (XSS) attack can be termed as an injection security attack through which an attacker injects malicious script into the victim's trusted website or web application. In an XSS attack, instead of targeting a victim directly, the attacker targets a legitimate website or a web application that the victim frequently visits. The attacker exploits security vulnerabilities in such websites to inject malicious scripts into them; the latter is ultimately delivered to the victim's browser when he/she visits the infected website or web application. Such a cyberattack can risk online business and client relationship miserably.

Did You Know?

Cross-site scripting (XSS) vulnerability is the most common vulnerability found in WordPress plugins.

Source: 'XSS Injection Campaign Exploits WordPress AMP Plugin'. https://www.wordfence.com/blog/2018/11/xss-injection-campaign-exploits-wordpress-amp-plugin/

How to defend an XSS attack?

A user can reduce the possibility of an XSS attack in the following ways:

- All application points, acceptance of data must be applied with input validation and HTML escaping. A character escape means representing a character in source code using only ASCII characters. Therefore, HTML escaping implies replacing characters with their corresponding HTML entities; for example, & is replaced with &amp.
- The user must disable scripting when it is not required.
- Links that involve sensitive data information directly from a third-party webpage should not be accessed.

Cyber Crisis Management: Why Do You Need It?

Have you ever heard about data thefts? Have you heard about a virus attacking your system whereby you lose all your confidential and important data? Have you ever tried to find a one-stop solution to all cyberattack related issues? In today's world, cyberattacks have become a major hindrance to our lives and we can become a victim of it anytime—whether we are doing serious business or just browsing through our social media accounts. In such cases, when you know a cyberattack can prove a fatal blow to your life or business, you should get yourself equipped with a cyber crisis management plan.

A cyber crisis management plan is the most important asset that all organisations should have. With a plan in hand, you can easily respond to a fatal cyberattack and even recover from the damage 'like a pro'. A cyber crisis management plan can diminish data compromise of your clients, reduce the time required to recover and, most importantly, save your company's reputation.

How to Develop a Cyber Crisis Management Plan?

The three major requisites of developing a cyber crisis management plan are:

Prepare for the worst

> *A robust cyber crisis management plan requires three requisites:*
> - *Prepare for the worst.*
> - *Respond at the first instance.*
> - *Recover from the attack!*

To create or develop a foolproof cyber crisis management plan for your business, you need to make sure that you are prepared for the worst. When you're formulating a cyber crisis management plan, make sure that your team members know their roles intensively. Your team should include members from all the departments including communication, operations and IT. The planning should be well rehearsed by all the team members for swift action against any cyberattack, irrespective of their type.

Respond at the first instance

Once you realise that your systems are under a cyberattack, the first thing you need to do is to know the type of the attack and use preventive measures accordingly. Your response team should be quick and respond to any cyberattack as soon as they are alerted about it. If you ignore any symptom of a hazardous cyberattack, you might incur limitless losses and the whole idea of a cyber crisis management plan might fail. A cyber crisis management plan is not an affirmation to 100 per cent safety from an attack, but it is a preventive measure that basically controls the amount of loss that might be incurred from an attack.

Recover from the attack

After a cyberattack, the recovery process is most important as it assures that none of your important data is eliminated permanently. To ensure smooth recovery of all your document and essential data, it is important to keep a record of data that is stored in your device, or there is a possibility of it being destroyed in any incident of a cyberattack.

Investigate

Once you've managed to avert a cyberattack with your effective cyber crisis management plan, you should always investigate the whole incident. First, you need to know the loopholes of your network that might have caused the attack. Second, it is important to know the root cause of a system malfunction due to a cyberattack which can cost the organisation millions of dollars at times.

A major reason to investigate is to make sure that the same incident is never repeated. If the cause of such an incident remains unknown, higher are the chances that you might become a victim of such an attack again.

While investigating, make sure you adopt the following approach:

- *Question* your staff and IT department about how and when they came to know about the cyberattack.
- *Investigate* internally to find out whether or not any individual from your organisation is involved.
- Always *isolate* the affected system to make sure that investigation is transparent without any alteration, fix or patch.
- Once you have collected all the evidence, *analyse* to understand the intensity of severity, cause and the impact of the incident.
- Once you are done with analysing, make sure to *strengthen* your system's security and also enhance monitoring to avoid future incidents.
- Always *inform* your clients and stakeholders about the incident to make sure that no important data goes unnoticed, or else, recovery of such data might be impossible.

Cyber Incidents: In the World and in India

Even after maintaining and spending so much over cyber security, hackers do find a way to disrupt our systems and now governmental organisations and big business houses have become an easy target of cyberattacks. The main reason for concern is that now hackers are able to access confidential data related to countries; this is undoubtedly unethical and unjust. Data theft from a country's major governmental organisation can lead to a lot of unnecessary and dangerous outcomes; thus, the government should ensure that cyber security is held as priority to avoid some grave situations. Not only India, but also the countries around the world, should make themselves aware of the dangers of the cyberworld.

Cyber Incidents

- **Google China hit by cyberattack:** In 2009, Google China's headquarters detected a data breach and it was believed that it was to access Gmail accounts of various well-known personalities and advocates of human rights. Later, it came to light that many such Gmail accounts had been accessed without permission in the US and in Europe as well. It was speculated that the Chinese government was exclusively involved in this data-security breach.

- **One billion account details stolen from Yahoo:** In 2013, hackers managed to steal account details of 1 billion Yahoo users. It is considered one of the biggest data-security breaches in the history of cyberworld.

- **Hackers managed to steal €650 million from banks:** In 2015, attackers managed to steal customer data from over 100 banks and through malware, they accessed the customers' account details, ATM pins and even managed to transfer huge amounts of money. This cyberattack resulted in the loss of €650 million of the customers.

- **Indian Bank data breach:** According to revelations, in 2016, data of around 3.2 million debit cards were breached and it affected major banks such as Axis Bank, HDFC Bank and ICICI Bank.

- **WannaCry heard around the World:** WannaCry ransomware was one of the most devastating cyberattacks. In 2017, this ransomware attack hit almost 150 countries including India. It affected around 2,30,000 computers around the world including systems in hospitals and telecommunication departments of major world- renowned organisations. The primary motive of the attackers was to extract money in the form of bitcoins.

- **WikiLeaks CIA Vault 7:** In 2017, WikiLeaks published data stolen from the CIA. It contained extensive documentation of spying operations by the government agency and data-hacking tools. It was revealed that iOS and Android vulnerabilities and bugs in Windows had the ability to turn smart TVs into listening devices, and some revelations also speculated that it had the ability to track the device's location through Wi-Fi signals.

- **Macron campaign hack:** In 2017, two days before the presidential elections in France, the official emails of the then presidential candidate, Emmanuel Macron, were leaked in public; in France, campaigning for elections is barred two days before the election. In no time, Macron's party released a statement stating that the leaks wanted to disrupt the democracy in France.

Impact of Cyber Security

Entire businesses, governments and retail organisations are equipping their systems with cyber security to avoid massive cyberattacks. Cyber security is important for ensuring that the companies are not always under the threat of cyberattacks and that they can perform confidently. When a company is equipped with a robust cyber-security apparatus, it will be able to combat such massive cyberattacks and thus its work output will also improve.

According to security experts, in the near future IoT (Internet of Things), Artificial Intelligence (AI) and blockchain will largely impact the working of cyber security. Handling cyberattacks will become more difficult and maybe uncontrollable too. A cyberattack on your device is quite disturbing, but imagine your car getting hacked while you're driving, in the era of IoT. In this progressive era of the cyberworld, we can't deny that soon AI might take over the world. Security experts believe that IoT will definitely add mountains of challenges for cyber security. Most of the cyber-security tools, equipped on our devices, are capable of detecting the known cyberthreats; however, concerns arise regarding the threats which are still undiscovered and new.

Security experts believe IoT will add challenges to cyber security.

Today, cyber security in organisations is a necessity, not a choice. It plays a major role in the development of an organisation. A client of any organisation can only trust them if the organisation has a robust cyber-security apparatus in place.

Despite knowing all about the ill effects of not having secure cyberspace, most users tend to ignore cyber-security practices! It is no wonder then that the rate of cybercrimes has been rising exponentially since the past decade. So, the question that arises here is: how to successfully get the cyber-security message through to people? How to get them to treat cyber-security awareness seriously? How to make cyber-security awareness stick out? Let us see how, through one such example, in the following box.

How to Make Cyber-security Awareness Stick? Use Humour!

Instead of pushing cyber-security awareness down people's throats and still not making enough difference, an innovative way to get the security message through to people is by using humour!

This method of using humour in cyber awareness was tried and tested by the then director of security at Yell (now Hibu, a multinational Internet services company headquartered in Berkshire, UK), Phil Cracknell in 2012. Cracknell made some videos about cyber security using *Stars Wars* characters.

One video featured Darth Vader where he is at the reception and has forgotten his ID card, and he is doing the 'Don't You Know who I am?' routine. Two-minute videos of these kinds were made to highlight the importance of cyber security and circulated among new staff during their first week at Yell; they were a huge hit!

Now that we have understood how crucial cyber security is for the maintenance of integrity and development of an organisation, it is now time to know about the various aspects of cyber security, the most important being cyber-planning. Without adequate cyber-planning and formulating risk mitigation strategies, it is rather difficult, or, next to impossible to prevent a cyber-security threat. More on this in the next chapter!

2

THE NEED OF CYBER-PLANNING

As the world is increasingly interconnected, everyone shares the responsibility of securing cyberspace through effective cyber planning.

—Newton Lee, *Counterterrorism and Cybersecurity: Total Information Awareness*

What Is Cyber-planning All About? Do We Leave It to the IT Professionals?

Whenever the word cyber-planning crosses our minds, there is often a prevalent notion that it is for the IT professionals or somewhat related to computer-science graduates. Are cyber crisis management and cyber-planning only meant for professionals sharing such backgrounds? Our goal is to dispel your doubts and provide you with adequate knowledge about cyber-planning.

We begin this chapter with a quote by the renowned global chief information security officer at Société Générale International Banking, Stéphane Nappo, wherein he says, 'It takes twenty years to build a reputation and a few minutes of cyber-incident to ruin it all.'

The book, *The Great Pearl of Wisdom* written by Bangambiki Habyarimana, aptly states that 'The most successful men work smart, not hard.' As authors of this book, we emphasise that there lies no alternative to your hard work, but we also believe that any half-witted decisions pertaining to your hard work not only sends you back to zero but also shows how naïve you are when it comes to acting smartly.

The idea of cyber-planning is like a pair of locks that you put on your door every time you go out on a vacation.

The idea of cyber-planning is like a pair of locks that you put on your door every time you go on a vacation just to ensure that everything which is inside, stays exactly as you have kept it. Proper cyber-planning ensures that whatever you have in your system stays there and cannot be tampered with. Cyber-planning is a tool to keep all your information and data secure and away from the reach of any misuse or tampering via the Internet.

In recent times, cybercrimes are the biggest threat to the era of digitisation and the business industry, which is worth trillions of dollars. The failure to prepare against a cyberattack is no longer an option. A proper cyber-plan not only ensures safety of information and data, but also ensures financial security and helps in maintaining one's reputation in the digital age. The techniques that are being involved in the commission of cyberattacks are highly sophisticated and

The failure to prepare against a cyberattack is no longer an option.

instantaneous. A proper cyber-plan not only ensures safety of intimate information and data, but also the financial security of the enterprise. Further, it also helps to maintain one's reputation in the digital age.

How Safe Is the Internet Today?

> *Most of us are unaware about the existence of the deep web which accounts for 90% of the Internet!*

The Internet that we are accustomed to doesn't even constitute a major part of the entire Internet network. For an average Internet user, the major role is played by Google, Bing, Wikipedia, social-networking sites and a few other sites related to their specific field of work. All these constitute the part of 'surface web' and account for less than 10 per cent of the entire Internet. What most of us stay unaware of is the existence of the *deep web* which accounts for 90 per cent of the Internet and cannot be accessed by surface web crawlers. The deep web, also known as the invisible web, contains academic information, governmental information, databases, confidential documents, legal information and other records of utmost importance, which are kept out of the reach of the general public.

The deep web has a subset known as the 'dark web' or 'darknet'. The dark web is the storehouse of illegal information, drug trafficking, weapon trafficking, human trafficking and all the other illegal activities that can be conducted through the Internet. Hackers offer hacking services through the use of the dark web. The dark web is accessible using browsers like TOR (The Onion Router), which successfully hides the identity of the user leading to complete anonymity.

Cyber-policy expert Arzak Khan, global advocacy director at Internet Policy Observatory, Pakistan, has argued, 'Connecting any strategic infrastructure to the Internet makes it vulnerable to security threats and most government systems connected are extremely vulnerable to hacking, data leakages and hijacking.'

Consequences without an Active Cyber-plan

Any business or start-up, irrespective of its size and performance, is highly susceptible to cyberattacks. If you run any business without an active cyber-plan, it is very similar to storing your valuables in a safe without locking it.

Fate of your business without an active cyber-security plan

Did You Know?

In 2014, Lenovo intentionally included a program called Superfish into all of its devices sold between September to December 2014. Lenovo began shipping laptops quietly bundled with a software called Visual Discovery, a version of Superfish's ad-injector Window Shopper, customised for Lenovo. When Lenovo customers browsed the web and hovered over an image, the software would inject a pop-up ad for a similar product sold by one of Superfish's retail partners. This software increased the possibility of cyber threats to an individual's computer via the collection of sensitive private information like passwords and account details.

Source: 'Remember When Lenovo Sold PCs with Superfish adware? It Just Got a Mild Scolding from FTC'. https://www.theregister.co.uk/2017/09/05/lenovo_gets_wristslap_from_ftc_for_superfish_adware_debacle/

Every organisation is unique when it comes to its functioning and so is the nature of the breaches. However, there are certain common incidents that every organisation which does not take cyber-planning seriously, has to face. They are as follows:

- **Loss of reputation**: A single cyberattack or mishap is enough to cost your business a steep decline in the number of customers you have and the number of stakeholders the company possesses. Nobody wants to engage in business with an organisation whose security has been breached, especially if it leads to disclosure of private and confidential information. Loss of reputation not only leads to fewer customers but also affects the future growth and ability to attract new talents, supplies or even investments.
- **Theft**: A cyber raid on a large company or a bank is something which might require a very well-executed and sophisticated plan, but attacks on smaller businesses which are typically primitive and easier to penetrate, are something we are accustomed to. When committing cyber theft, the attacker's motive is not limited to just stealing money. The hacker with access to the stolen data may sell it in the dark web and earn more than what he would have gained by financially draining out your reserves. For instance, the 2015 'Hidden Data Economy' report by McAfee

> *Common incidents experienced by organisations which do not take cyber-security planning seriously are:*
>
> - *Loss of reputation*
> - *Theft*
> - *Financial losses*
> - *Fines/penalties*
> - *Below-surface costs*

Labs puts the value of login credentials to hotel loyalty programmes or online auction accounts up to US $1,400. Intellectual-property theft, which leads to loss of year-long efforts and money spent on research and development by companies, is also damaging.

- **Financial losses**: The most common motive behind almost all types of cybercrimes is the desire to obtain financial gains through the means of breach. For a small business, a financial attack may result in the winding up of the business. On the other hand, for a big corporation, it might result in losses running into millions. According to the reports of a 2018 survey of Kaspersky Lab on 'The Cost of a Data Breach', the cost of experiencing a data breach is $120,000 on a global average for SMBs (small and medium businesses), which is a 36 per cent increase from $88,000 in 2017.
- **Fines**: Let's take a moment and think of the fact that the hacker is not satisfied just by causing grave financial losses to the host but also ensures that he/she gets punished for exposing his/her system to vulnerabilities. The hacker often commits fraudulent and criminal activities through the host which further compels the victim to suffer even more by paying fines.
- **Below-surface costs**: In addition to the various existing costs incurred by a cyberattack, there exist various intangible costs that continue to plague the business long after the commission of such a cyber incident. In the case of smaller firms, they already face the challenge to ensure constant cash flow, which is further crippled by increasing insurance premiums or increased interest on unpaid debt.

The Need for Cyber-planning in the 21st Century

There are chances that you do not have a clear idea regarding what you need to protect and defend so as to ensure cyber security of your IT systems. It is possible that you might only be concerned about network intrusion. However, there are dozens of other cyber-security risks which you may overlook or not even be aware of! Thus, you must have an active cyber-security management plan to protect your IT network. If you rely solely on a reactive defence mechanism, chances of you successfully recovering your cyber network from the after-effects of a cyberattack are very less. We are not suggesting you draw a cyber Maginot Line to keep away cybercriminals, because it is sure to fail. Instead, we strongly suggest you adopt proactive measures to protect your organisation; the first step towards the same is devising a cyber-security strategy.

The thumb rule is to develop a robust cyber-security strategy.

Did You Know?

Law firms are attractive targets to hackers as they hold a potential treasure trove of valuable commercial information and intellectual property.

Source: 'Why Planning Is Key to Combating Cyber Threats and Attacks'. https://www.theguardian.com/media-network/media-network-blog/2013/sep/06/planning-key-cyber-threat-attack

In any war, it is the strategy which drives tactics; in case of cyber security, there is no deviation from this thumb rule. All the detailed planning, solution architecture, behavioural responses and processes should align with what is laid out in the cyber-security strategy. The existence of a cyber-security plan highlights the commitment towards protection, which would otherwise not have been observed. A cyber-plan is the ultimate tool when it comes to measuring the performance of an organisation. You can easily highlight your expectations about how you wish to perform against a challenge while outlining and understanding the approaches necessary towards meeting the desired result. Without a proper plan, you can never be confident about your security stance. The planning should be such as to expand to those areas where a threat has not been experienced yet. It is foolish to believe that tomorrow's attack will be the same as of yesterday.

Once you start to use a cyber-plan, it serves as a medium of trust for your business stakeholders. It appears to them as the highest level of security and safety and thereby ensures a healthy business relationship.

Also, a cyber-security plan is the very first step of an organisation towards an attempt to coordinate. Each and every individual in the company, irrespective of their area of functioning and expertise, are bound to share certain parts of their strategy at a higher level. This allows the defenders to collaborate and coordinate just like the attackers do. The only key is to ensure that not all strategy is generic or shared. A cyber strategy provides a language that can be transmitted to the consumer or end users thus enabling privacy, security and freedom from intrusions.

The Major Cyber-security Threats That Can Cause Irreparable Damage beyond Return

- **Bots and malware**: Every one of us has experienced the troublesome nature of malware in one way or the other. The restless hours of calling the helpline for help and running all around to get a remedy. Malware can include minute nuances like spyware, which allows the digital hacker to track your every move, even the password that you are typing. Malwares are often introduced into the system whenever we download it or are tricked to download it by accident. When malware is used by a hacker to remotely take control over the system of an individual and perpetuate financial crimes or attack, we call it a 'botnet' or 'bot'.
- **Spam**: Whenever we hear the word 'spam', it directs our thoughts towards that place of our email account, which we refrain from opening at all. The truth is spam not only clutters your inbox, but also carries a lot of potential to cause serious damage. Spam mails can contain links which might make you download computer virus. Spam can also be effectively used to gain control over one's account, thereby urging every person who is in the contact list one step closer to a cyber incident.
- **Hacked accounts**: In order to understand this, we need to first revisit the concept of 'phishing'. As mentioned earlier, it is a practice where the hacker creates an email ID that looks exactly like the replica of the original email ID, which is duly certified. Once the email using the replica ID is sent to the targeted recipient, the hacker might gain access to the recipient's personal

data and account and the hacker may ask for the recipient's personal information, which might include account number, passwords or transaction details.

Once such information has been procured, it is further used to commit financial crimes, which might include running up huge bills on the person who has been attacked. Phishing scams are successful primarily because they make proper use of social engineering techniques to create an illusion and gain a person's trust.

- **Unsecured wireless networks**: Most of us use wireless Internet networks at our homes and offices to connect with our smartphones, laptops, televisions, computers and tablets. What we fail to understand and ignore is that cybercriminals always look for access to our Internet connection. Once they establish a connection, it takes moments to gain access to our device and perform the intended harmful activities.
- **Data gone missing**: If we consider all the places where we carry our mobile devices such as laptops, tablets and smartphones, it is very easy to lose them. If the data on these devices are not properly encrypted using an algorithm, it becomes prey to cybercriminals. A report by the Ponemon Institute 2012 shows that more than 45 per cent of all data breaches at major companies are caused by the use of lost laptops and smartphones.

The Need of Cyber-planning in India

Whenever we compare India with the major global players, it is evident that India lacks significantly when it comes to establishing a proper cyber crisis management plan. There are primarily two aspects that separate India from the major global powers when it comes to data protection—design and density. India has always been an information exporter. All data is directed towards the West. This is primarily because of the social media and other platforms existing in the West, and the simultaneous lack of any serious attempts by the Indian government to restrict such flow of data.

Talking about the density of cyberspace, India has nearly 500 million users who use the Internet every day. It is crucial for us to understand that not all Internet users use the same devices for accessing the Internet. For instance, Apple's share of usage in the US is 44 per cent while in India it accounts for less than 1 per cent. The enormous gap between the securities offered by the cheapest phones readily available in the Indian market and the high-end smartphones make it practically impossible to set proper legal techniques and standards when it comes to data protection.

Then arises the problem of no control over the hardware that is used by the Indian Internet users as well as the problem of information being carried away by them. India's infrastructure is susceptible to all forms of digital intrusions, especially espionage, which involves the act of intruding into systems to steal strategic and valuable information.

Cybercrimes, referring to electronic fraud or other acts that might lead to criminal consequences, are intended to disrupt services or systems for a temporary or an indefinite period. Wars caused by large-scale and systematic digital assault on India's critical and valued installations are particularly worrying.

There is an urgent need to build up skills in this very sophisticated area of technology; this might equip us to critically inspect any intrusion before they are deployed and hamper the functioning of the industry and the critical infrastructure. While dealing with cyber security, we need professionals who showcase the five major functional areas of cyber security, defined and forwarded by the National Institute of Standards and Technology. These are: to *identify, protect, detect, respond* and *recover*.

Equipping employees with cyber-security management knowledge and proper skill sets is required.

An estimate by NASSCOM's (the National Association of Software and Services Companies—a trade association of the Indian IT and BPO industry) cyber-security task force highlights that by the end of 2025, India will require at least 1 million professionals who are highly skilled in cyber crisis management. The number of such skilled professionals is only 62,000 as of now. There is a need that industries, enterprises and companies should upgrade the skills of their cyber-security and IT staff by introducing short-term courses. The present scenario is such that India might require introducing cyber-security management as graduate courses in various institutions across the nation. Equipping employees, irrespective of their area of function, with a proper practical skill set is also required.

The floodgates of Internet have stayed open for the past few decades and cannot be closed now. We are practically dependent on the Internet for all our wants and needs or, let's say, we are drowning in the virtual sea of the Internet. If we wish to secure the 'digital front' of our nation, we should start by adopting the required cyber-planning skill sets and implementing them in the form of cyber-planning and cyber crisis management.

What Does India Require at This Moment for a Better Cyber-safe Future?

- **Air gapping:** Air gapping is a security measure that involves the act of isolating a computer or the network it uses and thereby preventing any external connections. An air-gapped system is physically segregated and incapable of establishing a connection either wirelessly or physically with any other device, ensuring complete isolation and protection.
- **Big data analytics**: It is a process by which data is collected, organised and analysed in large sets. This enables the user to keep track of useful information and look for any anomalies instantly, using a common platform.

Emphasis on cloud-computing techniques is what we can call the need of the hour if we want to protect and secure our data from being hacked into. According to the reports of the National Crime Record Bureau (NCRB), the following are the statistics of cybercrimes committed in the past few years:

Table 2.1 Statistics of Cybercrimes Committed in the Past Few Years

Year	Number of cybercrimes reported
2013	5,693
2014	9,622
2015	11,592
2016	12,217

The data shows that there is a 69 per cent increase in cybercrime from 2013 to 2014, a 20 per cent rise from 2014 to 2015 and a 5 per cent increase from 2015 to 2016. The staggering number of cybercrimes mentioned earlier highlights the need for securing cyberspace through effective cyber crisis management planning.

In this chapter, we intend to focus on cyber-security management of banks, start-ups and small-scale businesses. Let us begin by understanding the cyber-security management plans from the perspective of a bank.

Cyber Crisis Management from a Bank's Perspective

In 2016, the Reserve Bank of India introduced cyber-security guidelines mandating Indian banks to put in place a board-approved and robust cyber-security management plan. In doing so, banks must formulate a cyber-security policy elucidating the strategies containing an appropriate approach to combat cyber threats. Such a policy can deal with the various complexities and high-level risks associated with these kinds of attacks. The same must be communicated to the Cyber-security and Information Technology Examination (CSITE) cell of the Department of Banking Supervision, Reserve Bank of India for approval.

Cyber-security Policy to be Distinct from the Broader IT Policy/IS Security

Policy of a bank

In order to address the need of the entire banking system and its functioning to contribute to a cyber-safe environment, the cyber-security policy should be distinct and separate from the existing IT policies and Information Systems (IS) security policies.

Arrangement for continuous surveillance

There should be a trend of testing for vulnerabilities at reasonable intervals of time. The nature of cyberattacks is such that they can happen at any time and in any manner, and cannot be anticipated beforehand. Hence, it is mandated by the RBI that a SOC (Security Operations Centre) be set up at the earliest, at every bank. The SOC shall ensure that there is continuous surveillance and also keep a detailed track of any latest form of emerging cyber threats.

Ensuring protection of personal and confidential information of customers

Of late, banks not only depend on technology for their smooth functioning, but also provide customised and cutting-edge digital products and services to their customers. Banks, being in possession of such confidential data of its customers, should take appropriate steps to preserve confidentiality and integrity, irrespective of the fact that the data is stored in their systems or is in transit or with any other third-party vendor.

Comprehensively address network and database security

Incidents have highlighted the need to thoroughly review and monitor the network security in every bank. It has been observed that many times, connections to networks and databases are allowed for a specified period to facilitate some business or operational requirement. However, the same does not get closed due to oversight making the network/database vulnerable to cyberattacks. Thus, it is of utmost importance that unauthorised access to networks and databases is not allowed; if at all permitted, it is through well-defined processes which are invariably followed without any errors and faults.

Sharing of information on cyber-security incidents with RBI

It is often found that most of the banks are hesitant to share cyber-security incidents and mishaps faced by them with the RBI. It is suggested by the RBI that banks actively participate in the activities of their CISOs' (Chief Information Security Officers') Forum coordination organised by the IDRBT (Institute for Development and Research in Banking Technology) and report any cyber incident to the Indian Banks Centre for Analysis of Risk and Threats (IB-CART). These attempts will help the banks in obtaining information on collective threat and hence, figure out a common way to tackle them and prevent further attacks.

Cyber Crisis Management Plan for Banks

Considering that cyber threats are far more sophisticated and different from any other risk that a bank might face during its operation, the traditional BCP (Business Continuity Plan)/DR (Disaster Recovery) arrangements are not at all adequate and hence cannot be accepted for tackling cyber crisis. In India, a government entity, the Computer Emergency Response Team-India (CERT-In), has taken up radical initiatives in strengthening cyber security by providing proactive and reactive services and guidelines. The CERT-In has also developed the National Cyber Crisis Management Plan and the Cyber-security Assessment Framework, which must be referred to for guidance while formulating a cyber crisis management plan by different banks.

The banks need to devise an effective solution to prevent cyberattacks and to promptly detect any cyber intrusions. Banks should be well equipped and are also expected to be well prepared to face emerging cyber threats such as 'zero-day' attacks, targeted attacks and remote access threats.

Cyber-security Operations Centre

The conventional security systems have always focused on preventive approaches and are generally reactive in nature. They come into play when the attack has occurred and its detailed information rests with the bank. As of now, the threat landscape has changed dramatically and hence, the method employed for handling threats needs a radical transformation. There is a need to take into account proactive approaches rather than depending on the reactive approaches of the past. This is the time when Cyber SOC comes into play. It considers proactive monitoring with the use of sophisticated tools for detection and quick response and is further backed by data and sound analytics. In the SOC, the system implemented to monitor the security takes into account a vast collection of logs from each point deployed, storing and processing the logs, correlating them through the required SIEM (Security Information and Event Management) tools and robust monitoring of SIEM screens in search for abnormalities. If any anomalies are found, the alarm is raised.

Cyber SOC has the following features to counter cyber-security attacks:

- **Methodology to identify** the primary cause of attacks, classifying them into pre-identified categories and coming up with solutions to contain further attacks sharing a common history.
- **Dynamic behaviour analysis** by conducting preliminary static and dynamic analysis, and collecting Indicators of Compromise (IOC). IOC are pieces of cyber forensic information which are found in system log entries or files, and which indicate the occurrence of a cyberattack.
- **Analytics** with a good dash board, showing the geo-location of the IPs in order to locate the place from where the attack is being conducted.
- **Counter response** and use the **honeypot services**. A honeypot network is used as a decoy system to lure hackers and other cyberattackers in order to detect and study the hacking methods for avoiding future attacks.

How Will the Banks Benefit from SOC

- SOC will help to protect critical business and customer data, demonstrate compliance with internal guidelines, country regulations and laws.
- SOC will provide real-time and instantaneous information on, and insight into, the security posture of the bank.
- SOC will enable to effectively and efficiently manage cyber-security operations by preparing for and responding to cyber risks and attacks. It will also facilitate continuity and recovery ability to assess

threat intelligence, and proactively visualise and predict its impact of threats on the bank.

- With the help of SOC, the banks will be able to preserve the information and evidence regarding the commission of the attack and every minute detail about the intruder.

Cyber-crisis Planning from the Perspective of Small-scale Businesses

There is a prevalent notion that just like the word cyber crisis management, people associate cyber-risks and attacks only with large businesses and corporate giants. Little do they know that out of all cyberattacks occurring worldwide the most vulnerable and attacked group is that of small-scale businesses.

Small-scale businesses are known to invest the major part of their profits for the purpose of their expansion without paying any heed to securing the cyberspace that is associated with the functioning of their business.

If we talk about the hackers, most of them love to attack small businesses. With minimum security deployment and operations being run on a modest budget, it ensures the absence of a proactive security policy. This leads to cybercrimes, such as stealing of valuable employee details, trade secrets, confidential customer information with ease. This enables us to directly reach a consensus that there is no point locking the stable after the horse has bolted. While dealing with cyber security there are no such shortcuts that ensure a proactive pre-emptive approach.

Here are certain factors that need to be considered if one wishes to avoid a cyberattack without shelling out a huge amount out of his pocket.

Is the website of the business protected?

Every business today—irrespective of its size, performance and progress—has one thing in common, that is, they have a website which educates their customers about their functioning and acts as a platform of exchange and financial transactions through portals. A hacker can successfully gain unlawful access over a website by exploiting bugs in the website server to execute malicious commands. The best way to avoid such an attack is to configure the server and software, without leaving any loopholes. Hardware is often used in the default way by small-scale businesses without customising and configuring it as per the security requirement. Once checked, the chances of cyberattacks are minimised.

Does the business put any emphasis on mobile security?

Mobile phones are the most frequently and prominently used device when it comes to any work that requires the use of the Internet. With the proliferation of mobility, many attackers have shifted their focus towards attacking mobile phones. Unlike other conventional systems, the fragmented Internet ecosystem along with varied operating systems and the extremely personal nature of configuration, make it almost impossible to develop a single strategy for tackling cyberattacks on mobile phones. So, if a business is not willing to lose its customers solely due to a cyberattack, there is a dire need for them to keep their website free from pop-ups and links that would surely lead to cyberattack. On the part of the customers, there is a need of awareness amongst the people giving up the use of unsecured Internet networks and public Wi-Fi as these ensure a large loophole for hackers to exploit. In order to fill the breach, one can encrypt all sensitive data.

Is the data encrypted?

Encryption can be defined as the emerging Holy Grail of cyber security. Encrypting data ensures that the cyberattacker is unable to conduct any attack unless they get access to the encryption key. Financial institutions and large-scale businesses have already encrypted their data. It is high time that these small-scale businesses also encrypt their data and make it an integral part of their operations. Small businesses would do well if they consider proper information processing certified encryption standards. Such standards ensure effective functioning and robust protection without being much heavier on the pocket. If we talk about operating systems, most of them come with encryption. For example, Windows operating system comes with BitLocker and Apple provides its users with FileVault. Activating these operations takes a few minutes and encrypts every file on the drive.

Does the business take backups?

Small-scale businesses will surely perform well if they backup all its records on a systematic and regular basis. During the case of a ransomware attack, the attackers hack and take control over the entire system. They then demand money for the decryption key. If there exists a backup in place, the business cannot do anything about the attack, but then it can restore everything leaving the attacker in complete bafflement. The businesses should also deploy encryption, password protection and other security measures to protect and safeguard the backup.

Does the employer give due importance to physical security?

Most of the small-scale businesses will argue that cyber threats only come via the Internet. What they essentially fail to understand and remain oblivious to are the dangers arising from the physical form. If a cyberattacker gets hold of the system used by an employee, a supplier or a physical agent, he can easily infiltrate into the system without actually hacking it. Mobile phones and laptops are also vulnerable to theft when the employee is constantly moving. What is required is a central security system that protects all such devices that are used by employees for business purposes; employees should be discouraged and penalised if they conduct any work through their personal devices—they must stick to office-supplied devices. The devices should again be deployed with proper tracking software to retrieve them in case of misplace or theft. It is quite common that sensitive information, due to the carelessness of employees, ends up in the trash can. This is a mine of opportunity for the attacker who constantly scourges trash for such information. Invest in a good shredder to enable the proper disposal of e-waste.

Does the business take emails and any other form of social threat seriously?

A large proportion of hackers introduce malware into the system, using email, phishing, spoofing and through infected applications. If a user clicks on a link sent through any of these, the user breaches the security protocol and downloads malware into his/her system. Such malware, after getting into the system, provides the hackers with remote control capabilities. The links can also lead to the installation of spyware and adwares, which send further pop-ups and redirect the user to certain websites and monitor the browsing activities of the user. If keyloggers are introduced into the system, then it can transmit sensitive information such as passwords and account numbers by gaining a command over the keyboard functioning.

The only way to tackle such attacks is by educating the employees about the hazards of opening spam mails and encouraging them to only open mails received from a verified source. The small-scale business owners should emphasise on installing strong spam filters to check suspicious mails and should block them instantly.

Does the owner of such small-scale businesses identify the possibility of rogue insiders?

In the era of intense competition, every businessman wants to gain an upper hand over the other. For this, they not only resort to healthy competition but take up immoral ways too. This might be simply achieved by paying a bribe to the employee or by assuring him a brighter future with a better pay scale. The loyal employees of a company might turn rogue if any mishap or misunderstanding occurs and hence, there is a need to check such vulnerability as this potential threat can come from any direction. In order to avoid any such mishap, the owner of a business should limit access to the employees. The best security protocol, in this case, will be based on privileges. In this, an employee only gets access to such files and policies, which he requires to carry out his work. No employee can share his password or acquire access to the entire system. Creating a security checklist for departing employees is also very essential. It is also the duty of the employer to secure all devices assigned to an employee before accepting a resignation.

An effective cyber-security policy means paying attention to such minor and often overlooked finer points. While they may seem insignificant and are often overlooked, such minor gaps are what that hackers wait to exploit and attack.

Cyber Management from the Perspective of Start-ups

As you read through this chapter there are bunches of people from every nook and corner of this planet planning their start-up. It's true that having a revolutionary idea is important, but is it all that you require? How to ensure the stability of your start-up and ensure that it finds itself a place in the future and isn't lost like the many which mushroom up and perish every now and then?

You might argue that your start-up is in no way a tech startup but you have documents to store and emails to send in order to communicate with your customers; you have financial records, intellectual properties, marketing strategies, budgets and what not on your system. All these are inherently important to you—and perhaps, can be even more valuable to someone else.

While you toil day in and day out, the hacker monitors and mirrors the progress. The start-up gets funded and your team is close to the final launch, you file the patent application and find there is already an identical product available beforehand. The hacker has successfully done his job and leaves you at zero. Therefore, you need cyber-planning irrespective of the nature and size of your start-up.

To protect itself from cyber threats, a start-up should adopt and implement various activities that ensure cyber security of its entire IT infrastructure. These activities constitute a very important part of the cyber-security management plan of a start-up and, if enforced regularly, can help a start-up prevent a cyberattack. The following box enlists such security activities that a start-up should undertake to maintain its cyber security.

Security Activities That Start-ups Should Implement

- There should be a risk or vulnerability assessment on a yearly basis along with key controls for high-risk assets.
- There should be endpoint security protection on desktops, laptops, mobile devices and any other device that is connected for work purposes.
- There should be security scanning of high-value assets, both at network level and at the application level.
- There should be security monitoring for assets that have sensitive data or intellectual information.
- There should be stronger and more effective authentication processes for privileged and high-risk accounts.
- There should be BCP (Business Continuity Planning) for critical processes.
- There should be information-security awareness and training for all employees and trainees as well as for any interns working in the start-up.

Did You Know?

A business turns vulnerable as soon as you make a mail ID for it.

Source: 'How I Hacked Hundreds of Companies through their Helpdesk'. https://medium.com/intigriti/how-i-hacked-hundreds-of-companies-through-their-helpdesk-b7680ddc2d4c

Myths Related to Cyber-planning Busted

When our discussion is related to cyber security, we should primarily understand that it is not a closed world consisting of only geeks and hackers. It is a modern-day concern that affects every one of us with or without our knowledge. Here are lists of a few myths that often keep us ignorant about cyber-planning.

Myth 1: Cyber security and planning has nothing to do with me

Individuals owning small businesses, companies and other ventures often believe that cyber-planning plays no role in their work. This is a major misconception. Whatever might be the nature of your work, once you keep vital information on a system and make transactions through the Internet, you are prone to cyberattacks. There is a prevalent misconception that if you access safe websites, then you are at no risk of facing a cyberattack. However, hackers can install malwares on such safe websites making you prone to cyberattacks without even clicking on anything. People often tend to believe that a strong password is all that they need to keep their confidential details safe. If one site is hacked, a cybercriminal can easily access all other connected accounts and thereby obtain access to all related information.

One might not be aware that even clicking on a mail from an unknown source that the hacker has camouflaged as a known source, opens a floodgate to cyberattacks.

We tend to assume that whenever we use a social-network platform, we are safe. The reality is that just like any other website, social media websites are vulnerable or rather more vulnerable as they act as a favourite playground for cybercriminals.

Myth 2: Affording a cyber-management plan is a costly affair

Everybody thinks that a cyber-management and security plan is too expensive to afford. The truth is that there is no doubt that it is costly. However, if you compare it with the price of getting hacked and losing all sensitive data and information which might force you to wind up the business, then the math becomes clear. A cyber-management plan is like a timely investment that ensures that you aren't tricked or attacked thereby protecting your information and enabling smooth conduct of your business and personal activities.

Myth 3: My antivirus software/firewall will protect my information

Gone are the days when antivirus software was all that you needed in order to protect your system and information. The present scenario is such that software alone will not stop cybercrimes, even a little. The false sense of security fostered in the minds of the users of such software highly exposes them to sophisticated attacks and enables the hackers to identify their easy prey. The antivirus software can help a little to contain damage once an attack has occurred but under no circumstances can it prevent such an attack. The promises of antivirus software have often lulled thousands of organisations around the globe, thereby making them the bigger targets.

Myth 4: We don't keep credit-card information on file, so we're not at risk

Credit-card fraud is perhaps the most common cyberattack that people face both at the individual as well at the organisational level. It is true that hackers are after credit-card data, but that's not their only target. Hackers might procure personal information, such as social-security numbers, bank account details, passwords, transaction details, etc.

Myth 5: I only download from trusted sources

Every person who doesn't want to invest in a cyber-plan will argue that he/she only downloads items from trusted sources. Ask the same question to a company until they find out that one of their employees clicked on the wrong mail and it brought a series of misfortunes to the entire company. Now the question is who takes the blame? The employee who clicked on the wrong mail or the company which decided not to invest in a cyber-management plan? The best way to avoid such a situation is to invest in a cyber crisis management plan.

Myth 6: Software updates are not essential, usually

The WannaCry attack in May 2017 is an evident example of what happens when you don't update the software.

Prior to the attack, Microsoft released an update to fix the vulnerability that WannaCry was designed to exploit. If an organisation takes months to patch vulnerabilities, there's enough time for the hackers to play their game while you are lost in procrastination.

Thus, it can be safely concluded that cyber-planning plays a very important role in preventing an organisation or an individual from a cyberattack. However, cyber-planning alone cannot resist a cyberattack. An organisation must implement prevailing cyber-security laws and policies in order to tackle cyberattackers. The following chapter deals with various laws and policies relating to cyber-security in select countries.

3

ORGANISATIONS, CYBER SECURITY AND THE LAW

it is often said that prevention is better than cure. But, we cannot always guarantee the non-happening of a mishap based on the preventive measures or precautions that we have taken. From what we have read in the last two chapters, we now have a clear understanding of why we need a well-planned cyber-security system. To draw a comparison—cyber security is the *prevention* while cyber law, commonly known as Information Technology Law, is the *cure*. In this chapter, we will deal with cyber crisis management within an organisation and the technical precautions that we must take in order to avoid a cyber incident. In the latter part of the chapter, once we have understood the concept of cyber crisis management, we will look into the laws related to these issues.

Cyber crisis management is a complex system which has information management, data privacy and cyber security as its integral essentials. Here, information management involves the collection and processing of information which is then filtered and categorised. Confidentiality is maintained by the element of data privacy; thereafter, a system called the cyber-security system is created to secure the managed information from external and internal threats. A strong nexus between these three elements facilitates cyber crisis management.

Let us start by looking into the essential elements of an efficient cyber crisis management system of an organisation.

What Do We Mean by Information Management and Data Privacy?

> *Cyber Crisis Management = Information Management + Data Privacy + Cyber Security*

Information management is the method of collecting, processing and condensing information with technological guidance, theoretical sophistication and human assistance. It includes the collaboration of both electronic and physical information. It is a broad term that incorporates systematic policies and procedures by the joint effort of the people in the organisation, including the technical and strategic decisions taken by them.

Basically, the management information system, which is popularly known as MIS, is a collection or storage of information and data relating to an organisation's field of work. This information is intrinsic and essential to the smooth functioning of the organisation. The system also has an element of data privacy which protects valuable information from being exposed. It is then further secured with the system of cyber security so as to make it inaccessible to viruses, hackers, malware and other forms of cyber threats.

Information management and data privacy go hand in hand in the sense that if the information that has been filtered and saved is not protected by cyber security, then it is exposed to internal, external and foreign threats.

The main factors that contribute to a successful information-management system are:

- People
- Process
- Technology
- Content

Role of people

Most of us might be familiar with one of the most famous dialogues of Bollywood actor Shah Rukh Khan in the popular movie *Chennai Express* where he says, 'Don't underestimate the power of a common man!' Rightly so, the people of any organisation is its most precious asset. An organisation, whether a boutique firm or a big company, requires efficient managing officials to run the firm smoothly.

When it comes to managing information, there are three broad categories of people:

- *Business managers*
- *IT security managers*
- *IT managers*

When it comes to managing information, there are three broad categories of people:

- **Business managers**: Business managers supervise the activities of employees, for which they hire, train and evaluate them; they simultaneously ensure that a company or department is on track to effectively meet the goals of the organisation. They also seek information related to budgets and thereafter prepare and maintain reports in accordance. These reports are then filtered and categorically saved in the server for future reference.

- **IT security managers:** IT security managers are officers of the organisation whose sole responsibility is to protect the entire IT network of the organisation, including computers. His or her job is to protect the organisation from software threats, such as computer viruses, data-security breaches, etc. These managers play a key role in avoiding cyber disasters by identifying them well in advance and formulating policies for safeguarding any weak areas that might make information systems vulnerable.
- **IT managers:** IT managers are responsible for the overall networking of the entire IT department of the organisation. They are also responsible for the performance of the Information Systems (IS) across all departments of the organisation. The main focus of an IT manager is to select the hardware and software required for the smooth functioning of the organisation, and also for enabling measures to increase the overall productivity and efficiency of the organisation.

Role of process

Business process is a collection of related and structured activities that are in a sequence. A business process is usually identified as a flowchart of a sequence of activities with relevant rules based on data in order. Business processes are beneficial to the organisation as they improve customer satisfaction and enhance the capacity for reacting to rapid market changes in an orderly fashion.

Role of technology

Technology has been a continuous asset to the organisation. Advancement of information includes constant acquisition of new technological products, which determines the stability of the technological infrastructure by supporting the organisation's information-management system, and thereby optimises business processes and delivers benefits.

Role of content

Management of content involves strategies, policies of information technology and information-systems opportunities, which improve differentiation and competitiveness. Strategic analysis tools, such as the value chain and the critical success-factor analysis are directly dependent on proper attention to the information that is (or could be) managed.

What Is an Ideal Data-management System?

So far, we have dealt with the different elements of managing information and data privacy. Any organisation that seeks to promote and follow an ideal data-management system needs to keep the following points in focus:

- **Information protection:** This involves securing data and saving it for later utilisation. Organisations should first decide on what kind of information they are looking for to protect and then develop a system for their protection accordingly.
- **Accessibility of information**: The organisation has to also look at whether the information that is available on its internal system is easily accessible, and whether

there are sufficient security practices deployed to protect the same and opt for measures of safety for it.

- **Evaluation of cost**: The organisation should also evaluate the relevant cost involved in protecting its vital information, thereby, generating budgetary appropriation.

What Are the Measures That an Organisation Can Take to Enhance its Information-management System?

Adoption of certain measures is likely to result in the enhancement of the information-management system of the organisation.

- **Taking backups and recovering them** include duplication of data in protected folders and recovering these folders in hours of crisis.
- **Archiving of information** is the process of moving data that is no longer actively used to a separate storage device for long-term retention. Archived data consists of older information that is still important to the organisation and may be needed for future reference as well as data that must be retained for regulatory compliance.
- **Disaster recovery simulation** involves simulating the actions following a disaster situation, using materials and equipment provided for at the recovery location.
- **Encryption of vital data** means the translation of data into a secret code which is known as encryption. It is the most effective way to achieve data

> *Manage and protect your information better!*
>
> *Backup, archive, encrypt and have a disaster-recovery plan in place!*

security. To read an encrypted file, we must have access to a secret key or password that enables us to decrypt it.

IT Security = Cyber Security

Cyber security, which is also known as IT security, is the protection of computer systems from theft or damage to their hardware, software or electronic data, as well as from disruption or misdirection of the services they provide. In spite of taking all precautions, that is, management of information, privacy of data and a fantastic system of cyber security, cybercrimes are still committed which cause great harm to individuals and organisations.

Tips for Information Management

- Organise a system's penetration test. These tests help in detecting the loopholes in the cyber-security system.
- Simulate crisis situations through interactive training programmes which act as examples of threats in a simulated environment.
- Advise employees with daily examples of security lapses, especially, those who are peculiar to your industry.
- Continuously update employees regarding subjective knowledge and trends with regard to information management.

Source: 'Security and Privacy Controls for Federal Information Systems and Organizations'. https://nvlpubs.nist.gov/nistpubs/specialpublications/nist.sp.800-53r4.pdf

How to Tackle Cybercrimes: Cyber Law!

Cybercrime, as a concept, has not been defined in any one particular fashion. It can be understood to be the illegal

Internet-mediated activities which occur across all nations and through global electronic networks. Existing laws in many countries are not framed to deal with cybercrimes which give the criminals an easy vacuum to commit crimes on the Internet. They take advantage of the gap in the law and our inability to track them down hastily. Cybercrimes not only mess with an individual's data but also put the economic strategies, political decisions and the safety of the nation at risk.

Only recently, with the boom of the Internet and sections of society understanding the working of the cyberspace, governments have been pushed to formulate laws regarding these crimes that are committed behind closed doors.

It is also necessary to understand that cybercrimes are not restricted to one country. The Internet is a vast forum and the crimes committed in that space can spread across borders and barriers. It is a global nuisance and thus requires absolute international cooperation among countries with the best interest in view. Various governments have already made joint efforts in establishing global standards of legislation and law enforcement both on a regional and on an international scale.

The 'Internet Century': Cyber Laws Across the World

The 21st century is often referred to as the Internet Century. We can hardly function without actively scrolling through our social media platforms or otherwise being online on the Internet. As they say, 'the Internet has immense power; the power to make or break people'. The Internet has a great impact on individuals and organisations in terms of social and political decisions.

Uncle Benjamin Parker wisely said, 'with great power comes great responsibility', and it holds true for cyberspace as well. The increasing popularity of the use of the Internet has, unfortunately, led to the exponential rise of cybercrimes on this platform. This global menace can vary from something as minor as cyber bullying to something as grave and serious as cyber terrorism.

We have already had our understanding of the fact that cybercrimes are not well defined, and even though the countries have underlying laws, the various types of crimes with their evolving nature make it extremely confusing.

Let us now, therefore, look at the most significant laws that our favourite countries have adopted. So, the next time you are faced with such a terrible crime, you'd know how to deal with it at the basic level.

United States of America

The US is one of the worst-affected victims of cybercrimes but it also has one of the strictest frameworks of cyber laws in action. The first-ever law to this effect was formulated in 1984 known as the Computer Fraud and Abuse Act (CFAA). However, the act did not include a provision for the intentional harming of devices by using malicious codes; this entails that the act did not include the idea of viruses.

Did You Know?

The US has been the most-affected country in the world in terms of Internet-related crimes with 23% of world cybercrime rate.

Source: 'Top 20 Countries Found to Have the Most Cyber-crimes'. https://www.enigmasoftware.com/top-20-countries-the-most-cybercrime/

The National Information Infrastructure Protection Act was legislated in order to form a more wholesome law. It included all the previous statutes and, additionally, held it illegal to view computerised information without authorisation.

The US has also excelled in terms of taking strict action against cybercriminals. Penalties like expulsion for criminal misdemeanour, felony and cyber bullying or 15 years of imprisonment and fine for identity theft or penalty of 6 to 20 years prison time for hacking and damaging computer properties. This demonstrates that the US has quite a stronghold on its cyber laws.

China

In the year 1997, the Computer Information Network and Internet Security, Protection and Management Regulations codified by the state council came into being in China. This was the first-ever law in relation to cybercrimes.

As per the Chinese criminal law, a minimum of three years of imprisonment has been specified for crimes constituting hacking, sabotaging data or creating and propagating digital viruses. The sentence can be increased as per the seriousness of the case.

The government of China has absolute control over the Internet within their borders since 2010 and while this may appear unfair and ridiculous to us, it has proved to be beneficial for indigenous e-commerce and digital companies of China.

India

Three per cent of the world's total cyberattacks are faced by people in India. The Information Technology Act of 2000 and its consequent amendments are the only strong laws that have been enacted in India to deal with cybercrimes. The law takes into account various crimes, such as violation of privacy, identity theft, sending of obscene material, child pornography and cyber terrorism.

Did You Know?

Almost 40% of the cyberattacks in India from January–May 2018 originated from China, 25% from thc US, 13% from Pakistan and 9% from Russia, according to CERT-In.

Source: 'Cyber Attacks Becoming More Frequent in India'. https://www.hindustantimes.com/india-news/cyber-attacks-becoming-more-frequent-in-india/story-8Os6AtCrHzL6QCBinVQuSM.html

India has also framed strict punishments for these crimes. Penalties of up to ₹2 lakh and imprisonment for heinous crimes, such as violation of privacy, have been formulated in the act. Fines of up to ₹10 lakh and up to five years' prison time for creating and sharing child pornography and lifelong imprisonment for cyber terrorism have been specified. These laws are quite strong if executed in an efficient way.

A crime-free society is a perfect dream and exists only in illusion. It should be our constant and conscious effort to keep criminalities at their lowest. In a society that is becoming increasingly dependent on technology, crimes in cyberspace are bound to rise and the lawmakers have to walk the extra mile to keep them afar.

In this century, where our world revolves around technology, we have to face the harsh truth that it is a double-edged sword and can be used for both purposes—good and bad. It is up to us to accept it as a boon or a bane. We, as a society, need to be more aware and ensure that technology grows in a healthy manner and is used for legal and ethical business growth and not for committing crimes and bringing others down.

Let us now look into a case which illustrates the necessity of having a cyber crisis management plan within an organisation.

Case Study

The **Bangladesh Bank heist** in 2016 was one of the most notorious cybercrimes in history, and the shocking part was how the attackers successfully intruded into the Society for Worldwide Interbank Financial Telecommunication (SWIFT), one of the most trusted, reliable and secure financial networks worldwide. It is a global network enabling financial institutions across the world to send and receive critical information regarding financial transactions in a secure standardised environment.

The timeline of the breach is as follows:

15 May 2015: With an initial deposit of $500, three bank accounts under the names of Enrico Teodoro Vasquez, Michael Francisco and Alfred Santos Vergara were opened in the Jupiter Makati branch of the Rizal Commercial Banking Corporation (RCBC), Philippines. These bank accounts remained idle until 4 February 2016 and were later discovered to be hoax/fake bank accounts.

January 2016: The cyberattackers injected malware into the bank's system.

4 February 2016: Attackers used the malware to hack into Bangladesh Bank's vostro account with the Federal Reserve Bank of New York (the Fed), and ordered 35 transfers worth $951 million, the bulk of which was to be transferred to the RCBC bank of Philippines. However, 30 out of 35 of these fraudulent transfers were successfully blocked by the Fed, but the remaining five transactions worth $101 million could not be blocked.

5 February 2016: The Fed sought clarification from the Bangladesh Bank regarding the 35 transfers, but failed to get through since it was a banking holiday in Bangladesh.

5–8 February 2016: The remaining five non-blocked transfers were executed. However, one transaction worth $20 million could be recovered owing to the discovery of a typographical error. One of the routing banks (also called intermediate banks), Deutsche Bank, blocked a transfer to a fake Sri Lankan NGO when it discovered the misspelling 'fandation' instead of 'foundation' in 'Shalika Foundation'. It was found that no such NGO existed in Sri Lanka. Unfortunately, the remaining $81 million were successfully stolen and routed to sham accounts in RCBC, Philippines.

8 February 2016: A 'stop payment' order was sent by Bangladesh Bank to RCBC. However, RCBC could not respond owing to a Chinese New Year holiday in the Philippines.

9 February 2016: RCBC permitted withdrawals from the accounts. Thereafter, the stolen money was consolidated and deposited in a dollar account which was opened on the same day under the name of William So Go of DBA Centurytex Trading. In the next few days, the money was successfully laundered to casinos in Philippines.

Possible measures suggested by cyber-security experts which could have thwarted the attack:

- Hackers broke into the perimeter network; stole local administrative credentials from hacked machines; used such stolen privileged local administrative credentials to search and move laterally throughout the environment until they found the SWIFT network; installed monitoring system on SWIFT-connected systems using such local administrative credentials; learnt how the SWIFT platform worked and accessed the digital certificates necessary to authenticate to the SWIFT network.

  All of this was possible because of local administrative rights. Therefore, standard business users must never be granted complete local administrative rights. Instead, a system must be in place that removes local administrative rights but enables users to elevate privileges as and when needed for approved tasks.

- Credentials of privileged accounts must be centrally secured; access to these credentials must be strictly controlled based on roles and approved tasks, and a multi-factor authentication process must be implemented before granting access to such credentials.

- All activities of privileged accounts must be subject to strict scrutiny and monitoring, since privileged accounts host and protect data and assets of the most sensitive nature. In the present case, if Bangladesh Bank had closely monitored the SWIFT account, it could have identified the anomalous activities, that is, the abnormal login patterns and prevented the attack.

- Organisations must segment off highly sensitive systems (such as the SWIFT network) from the rest of the IT network. This would ensure control and monitoring access and use, prevention of credential-harvesting techniques and better protection from malware infiltration from user endpoints to these sensitive systems.

- Organisations must enforce an application whitelisting policy which allows certain software programs to run while preventing others to do so. In the existence of such a system, Bangladesh Bank could have detected both the monitoring software and the malware in the SWIFT network.

The case mentioned earlier demonstrates the necessity of managing a cyber incident in order to successfully mitigate the adverse effects of, or altogether prevent the occurrence of, a cyber-security attack. Managing of a cyber incident and its utmost importance in protecting cyber security of an entity is discussed in the following chapter.

4

MANAGING CYBER INCIDENTS

In the previous chapters, we have discussed the importance of cyber security and the need for cyber crisis management in the world of digitisation. As the world is shifting towards digitisation to develop and make things easier for everyone, there are people who are trying to create problems for organisations by hacking their computer systems.

Not Possible to Secure Everything!

Cyber security plays a huge role in securing the data of an organisation. By this, we can secure our data to some extent but even after keeping layers of securities, we cannot ignore the fact that cyberattacks happen. It is not possible to secure everything. Despite adopting the best cyber-security practices, there are always chances that a cyber crisis may arise in an organisation. Proper management of such a situation is essential because it directly determines the chances of the organisation to recover from such a cyber incident and, in turn, its business continuity.

Need for Planning

To manage any situation, you need to plan for it in advance because these situations don't come knocking at your door to alert their presence. You need to ask the following questions: Where to start from? How to identify the problems? How to tackle those problems?

Stay calm at the time of a cyber crisis!

Once you have planned everything, you need to test to what extent your plan works whenever a cyberattack happens. You should know how to properly manage a cyber incident, which involves right decision-making at the right time. This decides the future of your organisation and would also help you to recover all the losses and damages.

How to Manage a Cyber Incident?

Somebody must have advised you to stay calm in difficult situations at some point in your life so that you can take the right decisions. Similarly, it is very important to stay calm at the time of a cyber crisis, if you don't want things to get worse. People tend to panic at this time and lose control of their minds, which only worsen things. So, it is very important to take the right decision to deal with the cyberattack.

Did You Know?

The amount of damage done by data breaches is stunning! In 2017, 1,293 data breaches, responsible for exposing more than 174 million confidential records, was recorded in the US, which was 45% more breaches than 2016.

Source: '2018 Data Breaches—The Worst of Last Year'. https://www.identityforce.com/blog/2018-data-breaches

Every organisation has its own way of dealing with cyber crises or cyber incidents; though some prove to be successful and some do not. Here are some steps that could be taken to deal with a cyber incident:

- **Inform everyone**: The very first thing one should do is to inform everybody working in the organisation about the incident. A team of specialists should get ready to respond to it. The main goal in the beginning is to minimise the damage. The team should consist of people having sound knowledge of their respective roles, like the people who are appointed as cyber-security technicians should focus on the source of attack; people who are appointed as data-protection specialists should try to control the attack; client-service staff should inform the customers if their personal data is breached, etc. In short, each person should work according to their respective duties.

Did You Know?

The 2017 Annual Data Breach Preparedness Study of Ponemon Institute revealed that 88% of companies had a data-breach response plan in place, but only 49% viewed such plans as effective.

Source: 'Fifth Annual Study: Is Your Company Ready for a Big Data Breach?' https://www.experian.com/assets/data-breach/white-papers/experian-fifth-annual-preparedness-study-2018.pdf

- **Have a plan**: The next move of the team should be to find out the type of attack your organisation is facing, to know the impact and extent of damage and also the source of the attack. Once you get to know what actually has happened, then it gets easy to select the best action plan and then the whole process goes according to that.

- **Secure the network**: After identification of the attack, the next step is to secure the network to prevent the rest of the data from getting damaged. That might lead to system isolation from the network and other actions could be taken to block the hacker's activities, such as implementation of a temporary e-security patch or using temporary firewalls for the time being.

Did You Know?

According to a 2018 global study, the total average cost of a data breach rose from $3.62 million in 2017 to $3.86 million in 2018, which was a 6.4% increase. Plus, having an Incident Response (IR) team was identified as the top cost-saving factor, reducing the cost by $14 per compromised record.

Source: '2018 Cost of a Data Breach Study: Global Overview'. https://www.ibm.com/downloads/cas/861MNWN2

- **Detect and solve the problem**: The next course of action is to investigate the matter which would help in identifying the hacker. Ask questions like how he got access to the system and to what extent the data has been damaged. You could also report the matter to the cybercrime branch of law enforcement agencies in your area; this would help you to take legal actions against the cybercriminal after which you can start rebuilding your system and securing all the important data with enhanced security measures.

- **Rebuild your relationships with clients**: The most important thing after this is to manage the relationships with your customers and stakeholders because a cyberattack is bound to have created doubts in their minds, which means that the goodwill and reputation of your organisation are at stake. So, it is important to disclose the whole situation and assure them about the effectiveness of the recovery steps that you have taken, in order to regain their trust. Customer loyalty is crucial in maintaining the brand equity of your organisation, and vice-versa. Hence, you should take utmost care in rebuilding the same, and also ensure that your cyber-security measures are state-of-the-art and capable of preventing or detecting any future attacks.

Figure 4.1 Steps to Manage a Cyber Incident

Importance of Managing Cyber Incidents

It is common observation that an organisation does not pay attention to important things unless it affects its operations or it has suffered financial damage. Similarly, managing a cyber incident almost always signifies post-crisis management wherein

> *The manner in which an organisation deals with a cyber crisis determines its ability to regain customer loyalty.*

the cyberattack has already happened and now needs to be dealt with.

This is a very crucial part for any organisation since it decides the fate of the concerned organisation post-attack. The manner in which an organisation deals with a cyber crisis determines whether it will be able to continue its business operations and regain the loyalty of its customers, investors and other stakeholders, or it will succumb to the ill-effects of the cyberattack and never recover.

Did You Know?

According to a 2018 global research study exploring the factors and challenges of being a cyber resilient organisation, it was found that 77% of the firms that were surveyed lacked proper incident response plans; while 69% reported that funding for cyber resiliency was insufficient.

Source: 'The Third Annual Study on the Cyber Resilient Organization'. https://www.ibm.com/downloads/cas/D3RGN4AJ

An organisation should be ready at any given time to face and counteract cyber-crisis situations!

Hence, an organisation should always be prepared to face and counteract these types of crisis situations. Cyberattacks can happen with anyone and anywhere; so, it becomes very important to secure your IT systems with all possible security measures. Your readiness should be such that your security measures are able to counter an attack as soon as it happens without any delay!

Learn from Prior Cyber Incidents

> *An organisation should learn from its mistakes.*

They say that in life everything counts, and here, every decision counts because one wrong decision could damage the entire business, and that would directly lead to irrecoverable loss. So, you need to keep your eyes, ears and your mind open to take the next decision because the entire development of your organisation, its profit and goodwill depend on that.

It is said that people learn through their mistakes. Even if the organisation has secured its system with high security measures, there is always a possibility that such systems could be hacked. An organisation should always learn from the incident that happens with them. This will help them to acquire knowledge on methods of strengthening the security of their systems and the types of data which require more stringent security, in order to save their systems from getting hacked again.

Important Factors That an Organisation Should Consider to Manage a Cyber Incident

There are many additional details which an organisation should focus on to ensure the effective management of a cyber incident:

> *An organisation should conduct training programmes on cyber-security practices.*

- An organisation should organise training programmes for all the specialists and employees at regular intervals so that they are adequately aware of cyber incidents that have occurred in the recent past, and are able to acquaint themselves with and educate themselves on the measures to prevent or cope with such incidents.

- They should check to what extent their security measures are effective by conducting periodic tests. This would enable them to assess the strength of their current security systems and accordingly update and add necessary features to further strengthen it.
- An organisation should determine which type of data needs higher levels of security and accordingly provide layers of security since data of a more sensitive and confidential nature tend to get hacked more frequently.
- Maintaining strong password hygiene across the organisation could actually prevent attacks. So, an organisation should always use strong and different passwords for separate accounts. This is the simplest and very first step towards securing or protecting your data which the authorities should always keep in mind.

Did You Know?

In a 2017 research survey conducted by SecureAuth Corp, the market leader in adaptive access control, jointly with Wakefield Research, it was revealed that 81% of the people surveyed used the same password for more than one account; whereas 92% of millennials surveyed reported using the same password across multiple accounts.

Source: 'SecureAuth Survey: Majority Of Americans Reuse Passwords And Millennials Are The Biggest Culprits'. https://globenewswire.com/news-release/2017/07/19/1054094/0/en/SecureAuth-Survey-Majority-of-Americans-Reuse-Passwords-and-Millennials-Are-the-Biggest-Culprits.html

Worst Password Mistakes!

Las Gatos based cyber-security firm, SplashData, evaluates millions of leaked passwords every year to determine and provide a list of the most **easily hacked**, and thus, **worst-protected passwords**. The 2018 list includes:

123456	Password
123456789	12345678
12345	111111
1234567	Sunshine
qwerty	iloveyou
princess	admin
welcome	666666
abc123	football
123123	Monkey
654321	!@#$%^&*
Charlie	Aa123456
Donald	Password1
qwerty123	

Experts recommend using different passwords for different logins and passphrases of at least 12 characters with mixed types of characters such as numerals, alphabets in different cases and special characters.

Some Cyber Incidents from Around the World

Let us take a look at some cyber incidents from around the world:

Sony PlayStation network attack

> **Biggest Mistake**
> *Sony did not bother to protect their network!*

There are many organisations who do not use e-security or multi-factor authentication to protect their user accounts—this is a big risk taken by them. They feel that their conventional technique of securing the network is enough. But things went awry in the case of the Sony PlayStation network attack.

In 2011, hackers broke into the system and personal information of approximately 77 million accounts were hacked and published. The only resort left for Sony was to shut down their networks for a few weeks. Their only mistake became their biggest mistake ever—they did not bother to protect their network. Hence, they became the victim of a major cyberattack.

Hackers, who attacked the system, said that it was a very easy task as there was not much of security and their sole objective was to show how insecure Sony systems were. The most challenging phase for Sony was to gain the trust of their customers again and to reassure them that their data was safe with them after the incident.

Things to Learn from This Case

No one should ever think that just one layer of security is enough to protect their systems from getting attacked. As cyber-security measures are progressing with technology, even the hackers are updating their ways and techniques of attacking the system. So, one should always put on multiple layers of security since no one can guarantee the safety of their data. Hence, all possible ways of data protection should be implemented to minimise the chances of hacking.

Attack on the Maharashtra government's official website

In 2007, the official website of the Maharashtra government was hacked. The website obviously contained important information about sensitive state matters, confidential information of the department, critical reports, etc. In this case, the cybercrime branch in Mumbai was also involved as it was a big issue that a government site had been hacked. After the investigation, the officials revealed that the website had been earlier affected by viruses on multiple occasions. It was also discovered that the website had no firewall. This was followed by catching the hackers and getting the website on track.

Things to Learn from This Case

The risk of not protecting the website should never be taken especially when the website contains valuable information. In this case, it was revealed that the website was affected by virus attacks on several occasions even prior to the hacking incident. So, it is crucial that your IT systems have adequate safety measures which are capable of detecting any form of cyber threat or intrusion, and take immediate actions to stop further injury and contain the attack.

Uber case

It is safe to assume that we are well acquainted with Uber, a transportation network company. In 2016, Uber was hacked. Personal information of approximately 57 million users and 6,00,000 drivers was published. It was revealed that the manner in which the cyber incident was handled, worsened the after-effects of the attack. The breach was made public after a year of its occurrence. They even paid $1,00,000 to the hackers to destroy the data. Both their reputation and money were at stake.

Things to Learn from This Case

This case teaches us about the necessity of an organisation to handle a cyber incident efficiently. An organisation must respect the 3 R's of cyber crisis management: readiness, response and recovery.

The attack on JPMorgan Chase

JPMorgan Chase (JPM) is one of the largest banking institutions of the US. In 2014, JPM was hacked, which compromised the data of approximately 83 million accounts which included names, email addresses, phone numbers and other confidential information of the users. The hackers attacked the root of the system and executed activities, such as closing accounts or transferring funds. The hackers were caught and a case was registered against them.

Things to Learn from This Case

An organisation must protect its IT system in an efficient manner to avoid spilling of private and confidential information in the public domain or into the hands of unscrupulous elements.

The cyberattack on Bayer

According to reports, infectious software was detected on the computer networks of Bayer, a popular German manufacturer of drugs and pesticides, in early 2018. A hacker group known as Winnti was suspected to have conducted the cyberattack. Reports of Bayer's Cyber Defense Centre, however, stated that there was no evidence of data theft, and Bayer's cyber security was restored without any major damage. Prior to Bayer, the Winnti group was also reported to have attacked the cyber network at Thyssenkrupp, a renowned German technology group, in 2016.

Things to Learn from This Case

Any organisation, irrespective of its scale and size, may be victimised by cyber criminals. Thus, cyber security must not be taken for granted, and adequate steps must be taken to upgrade existing cyber-security measures of an organisation to protect its computer networks from vulnerabilities. It is possible to prevent damages caused by cyberattacks if they are detected and contained at an early stage, which can be achieved only if a strong cyber-security system exists in an organisation.

Facetime eavesdropping bug

Recently, a major security flaw was discovered in Apple's FaceTime. The bug, which was initially reported on 28 January 2019, allowed a user to eavesdrop on another individual via FaceTime by connecting the service's video and audio, even after the rejection of the FaceTime call by the other user. Apple has reportedly resolved the issue by releasing a software patch and conducting a thorough security audit.

Things to Learn from This Case

Organisations must act quickly in order to contain or mitigate cyber-security breaches. In the present case, further damage was prevented when Apple disabled its FaceTime services.

After reading the above cases of cyberattacks on various well-known and large-scale business organisations as well as on a government website, it is clear that organisations must implement cyber-security measures along with a proper cyber crisis management plan.

Major Cyber-incident Managing Mistakes

It is excellent to have a cyber-incident response team, but there are times when they could also commit errors and mistakes. You can formulate the best plan out of every available resource, but the success of such a plan depends upon how well-thought and practically executable it is.

The following box describes some major cyber-incident managing mistakes:

- The members of the cyber-management response team might be from different sections of the organisation. Since their way of working is different from each other, it is possible that they might have communication gaps and difficulties in coordinating with each other. In these situations, things often don't go as planned which ultimately defeats the purpose of the cyber-management plan. So, communicating with each other in the right way is very important at the time of crisis.

- When organisations devise a cyber-incident management plan, it is very important to assess whether such a plan is capable of being executed at the time of the actual incident. Therefore, it must go through several stages of testing. In the event of a failure, appropriate changes should be made along with recorded reasons for its failure and details of the new security features that were adopted.
- A major area of concern is manhandling of critical evidence by inept or inexperienced professionals. Appropriate personnel must be trained in proper ways of handling cyber evidence so as to prove incidence of the cybercrime and thereby convict the criminals responsible for such a cyber incident.
- Hackers often exploit lack of cyber-security awareness of Internet users to initiate and execute cyberattacks. It is, therefore, very important to educate users about the common exploitation practices and the role of information security so that they are able to avoid committing grave Internet security mistakes such as downloading files from untrusted sources, clicking on questionable pop-ups or maintaining poor password hygiene.

Did You Know?

In 2017, 91% of cyberattacks started with a phishing email.

Source: '91% of Cyber-Attacks Start with a Phishing Email: Here's How to Protect Against Phishing'. https://digitalguardian.com/blog/91-percent-cyber-attacks-start-phishing-email-heres-how-protect-against-phishing

Difficulties Faced by Small-scale Organisations During a Cyberattack

Small-scale business organisations usually tend to think that they are not prone to cyberattacks owing to their size as compared to larger corporations, but they fail to realise that hackers do not care about the size of an organisation. The aim of the hackers is to prove that they are capable of hacking into network systems of any and every organisation, big or small, and thereby, wreak havoc in the organisation by stealing, destroying or otherwise tampering with important confidential data and/or causing financial and reputational loss of the company.

Reasons why small organisations are more prone to cyberattacks:

- Small organisations generally avoid making cyber security top priority owing to huge expenses and complex data-protection regulations and almost always ignore it. They tend to invest in baseline security measures, which are child's play to hackers. They are often unable to afford highly sophisticated cyber-security protection systems, and hence, inevitably attract cyberattacks.
- Small organisations are often unable to afford expert professionals who could look after and upgrade their security systems at regular intervals to keep the data protected due to budgetary reasons. This leaves them more vulnerable and exposed to the danger of getting attacked and they are often unable to recover from such an attack due to lack of necessary resources.
- One of the reasons small organisations face frequent cyberattacks is because of their unaware and untrained staff. They are often unable to afford training their

employees on cyber-security maintenance owing to a tight budget. On account of this unawareness or otherwise negligent and callous behaviour, employees often click on malicious emails, questionable links or dubious pop-ups, thus instrumenting an intrusion and ultimately, an attack.

- It is quite common that hackers use IT systems of smaller organisations as vehicles to attack larger corporations because the IT systems of smaller organisations are interconnected with the information systems of large organisations. Hence, by breaking into the IT system of smaller organisations easily, they can easily break into the systems of large organisations.
- Ransomware attacks generally make the situation more vulnerable because small organisations are more inclined to pay ransom to save their lost data as well as their goodwill and reputation.
- Many small organisations have begun implementing the Bring Your Own Device policy (BYOD), thus allowing network connectivity on personal devices. So, it is very important to ensure that such personal devices are free from any intrusions and threats as well, because it is quite possible that hackers use these infected personal devices as a vehicle to institute attacks against the entire organisation.
- Small-scale organisations tend to ignore updating their systems or installing new software patches or bug-fixes. Outdated systems are more vulnerable and very easy to hack into or attack.

These factors could also be identified as reasons why small organisations are not able to grow, develop or increase their customers because how would any one place their trust in such organisations which do not have a good reputation, do not have their systems secured properly and which cannot guarantee the safety of their data and personal information. It's like wasting money even after knowing the consequences.

Did You Know?

According to a 2017 cyber risk report, on a global average, companies around the world take 146 days to detect a cyberattack whereas companies in the EU take 3 times longer than the global average—469 days to detect a cyber intrusion.

Source: '2017 Cyber Threats: A Perfect Storm About to Hit Europe?' https://www.fireeye.com/content/dam/fireeye-www/global/en/current-threats/pdfs/rpt-world-eco-forum.pdf

Tips for Small Organisations

- Small organisations should have a cyber-insurance policy which could help and protect them from incurring additional expenses associated with data breaches. For example, data recovery expenses, incident response expenses, etc.

Small organisations should have a cyber-insurance policy.

- Organisations should train their employees about cyber-security management. They should be ready to respond to any form of cyber threat and be able to recover lost data and information. If budget permits, these organisations should consider hiring expert professionals on a consultancy basis.
- Organisations should put layers of security on sensitive and more valuable data as per their budget.
- Organisations should develop effective cyber-security policies such as password management, educating

employees about cyber-security basics on a regular basis, telling them to limit their access to sensitive information, instructing them to keep all the software and applications up-to-date, etc.

- Ransomware is a big concern for such organisations because, in order to recover their data, they agree to pay ransom to the attackers. Therefore, an organisation should conduct regular data backups, have a decent malware-protection system and should educate employees about basic cyber-security etiquette.
- Every organisation should use https (hypertext transfer protocol secure) on their website because without it the hackers can easily see each and every information available on their website. The hypertext transfer protocol provides encrypted communication and protects the identity of a network web server.

Did You Know?

Cybersecurity Ventures, a leading researcher on global cyber economy, estimates that cybercrime damages will cost the world $6 trillion annually by 2021, increasing from $3 trillion in 2015.

Source: 'Cybercrime Damages $6 Trillion By 2021'. https://cybersecurityventures.com/hackerpocalypse-cybercrime-report-2016/

Let us now look into a case which shows that proper management of a cyber incident by an organisation is crucial to ensure its business continuity. An organisation of any size and nature may fall prey to a cyberattack, but the key to recovering from such an attack is to mitigate it efficiently using an effective cyber crisis management plan. The victim organisation may be a large corporation, but if it is unable to properly manage a cyber incident, chances are that it may never regain the loyalty of its customers/ other stakeholders, and in extreme cases, suffer losses huge enough to suspend/ shut down its business operations.

Case Study

The **DigiNotar** cyber-security attack in 2011 was one of the biggest digital disasters in the Netherlands. DigiNotar is a Netherlands-based certificate authority which was established in 1997. Also known as a Trusted Third Party (TTP), a Certificate Authority (CA) is entrusted with the task of issuing digital certificates after verifying the identity of the recipient (whether a person or an entity) requesting such a digital certificate. This implies that a CA guarantees the authenticity of a certificate issued by it, and such a certificate can be considered digitally safe and secure. In the present case, DigiNotar was responsible for issuing three kinds of digital certificates—standard, qualified and Dutch government certificates otherwise known as PKIoverheid certificates.

The timeline of the DigiNotar cyber-security breach is as follows:

17 June 17–1 July*:* Cyberattackers gain access to the internal network of DigiNotar systems by breaching the perimeter network.

10 July*:* Attackers generate the first fraudulent certificate.

10–22 July*:* Cyberattackers hack into all certificate-signing systems of DigiNotar and generate around 531 fraudulent/ rogue certificates for about 53 different Internet domains.

19 July: DigiNotar discovers a mismatch between issued certificates and its administrative records, and thus detects the attack. DigiNotar, however, keeps silent about the intrusion.

27 July–27 August: Fraudulent certificates generated by DigiNotar are used in Man-In-The-Middle (MITM) attacks on an estimated 3,00,000 users who were exclusively located in Iran. A MITM attack involves the attacker inserting him/herself into a conversation between two parties and by way of impersonating both parties, gaining access to information that either party means to be received by the other. This implied that the traffic intended for Google subdomains were redirected and intercepted using the MITM attack, thus leading to potential exposure of the traffic contents and Google credentials of all the affected users.

28 August: An Iranian user receives a warning from his web browser, Google Chrome, regarding the trustworthiness of the certificate when he tries to log into his Gmail account. The user notifies Google and upon investigation, it is found that the certificate is indeed corrupt.

29 August: The break-in is detected by Mozilla as well. CERT-Bund the German national computer emergency response team informs its Dutch counterpart, GovCERT of the attack. DigiNotar goes public about its cyber-security breach.
3 September: DigiNotar is officially renounced by the Dutch government as a trustworthy certificate authority.

14 September: Dutch authority on telecommunications revokes DigiNotar's license to issue qualified certificates.

20 September: DigiNotar files for bankruptcy due to irreparable damage of its trustworthiness in generating authentic digital certificates which was its primary business product.

Cyber forensics attributed the massive breach of DigiNotar to the following factors:

- DigiNotar failed to install anti-virus software on its (investigated) servers. This led to the presence of malicious software on its critical services, which could otherwise have been detected by anti-virus software.
- DigiNotar failed to install necessary updates and software patches on its public webservers, which are critical for maintaining cyber security. It was discovered that DigiNotar had neglected to install 30 critical software updates.
- DigiNotar failed to separate its critical components. Meaning, all its CA servers formed part of a single Windows domain, thus implying that all such servers could be accessed by only one username and password combination. Evidently, the single password failed to be strong enough to resist hacking of such a massive scale.
- DigiNotar exposed itself to cyberattackers due to the vulnerabilities resulting from its outdated software system. Further, DigiNotar failed to respond to initial signs of a targeted attack, which could possibly be averted if not for the major security flaw, that is, the outdated software.
- DigiNotar lacked adequate oversight, security attention, risk awareness and an effective cyber-security risk mitigation strategy.

Cyber Security Is a Never-ending Battle!

By now, we have understood that cyber security is a never-ending battle. There is no permanent solution to it as of now but we can fight against it by formulating appropriate cyber-incident response plans and accordingly implement them. Organisations should be updated on the latest hacking techniques, and they can accordingly secure their data and information. Therefore, managing a cyber incident is an ongoing process rather than a one-off incident.

A well-secured and strongly protected system is always a challenge for hackers as they have to spend more time hacking them as compared to weakly protected systems and thus have to try and initiate new techniques, which is very time-consuming.

> *Cyber security is an issue which needs interdisciplinary understanding from all spheres.*

Cyber security is an issue which needs understanding from all spheres, such as economics, organisational behaviour, sociology, engineering, law and not just information technology and computer science. Just as it is important to know about the technical aspects of a cyberattack, it is adequately important to know how a cyberattacker operates, such as the common or popular security vulnerabilities that most hackers usually exploit or what are the security measures which hackers have managed to bypass in the past.

It is thus of paramount importance that organisations, irrespective of their size and nature, have a cyber-incident management plan in place, to ensure smooth functioning of their business operations. Let us now understand the relation between cyber security and the Internet of Things in the next chapter.

5

CYBER SECURITY AND THE INTERNET OF THINGS

> *The term Internet of Things was first used by Kevin Ashton in 1999.*

We, as individuals, should have a fair idea about the Internet of Things (IoT) as a concept. IoT is a term used for a system digitally connected via the Internet, where the system includes a large variety of devices ranging from a desktop, a laptop, a television to a doorbell cam or even a wristwatch. In other words, IoT is a collection of devices which are digitally connected to each other for making our life easier. The term Internet of Things was first used in 1999 by Kevin Ashton. Ashton was a British technology pioneer and co-founder of the Auto-ID Centre at the Massachusetts Institute of Technology, which created a global standard system for Radio Frequency Identification (RFID).

As technology keeps improving our living standards, it simultaneously raises some serious security concerns vis-à-vis our data. In other words, technological advancement is also becoming a threat to cyber security as has been repeatedly discussed by us in the preceding chapters.

In this chapter, we will discuss how the Internet of Things has affected our lives both positively and negatively and what are the steps that can be taken to resist threats to cyber security through IoT.

How Can the Internet of Things Be Useful in Our Daily Lives

Internet of Things aims to reduce human labour and improve the standard of living through smart devices that work through software, sensors, actuators, etc. to connect to each other and share data. These smart devices capture the daily activities that we perform either online or offline and execute their tasks taking into account those activities of ours, thereby reducing our manual labour.

Important Facets of IoT

Let us now discuss some important facets of the Internet of Things. For instance, you can automatically open your garage door just a few minutes before you are about to enter it with your car; or, turn off the lights of your room, which you forgot to do, even when you are outside; or, unlock the door of your house for your relatives when you are not at home.

Did You Know?

According to Forbes, 87% of people actually have no idea what the IoT means or what it stands for.

Source: '17 "Internet of Things" Facts Everyone Should Read'. https://www.forbes.com/sites/bernardmarr/2015/10/27/17-mind-blowing-internet-of-things-facts-everyone-should-read/#2df6766d3505

All the above examples are the features of a smart home, which is the most-searched IoT associated feature on Google. A smartwatch, another popular IoT device, can help you measure your heart rate, how much distance you have covered in a day, your acceleration at a particular point in time, etc.

Figure 5.1 Evolution of Internet of Things

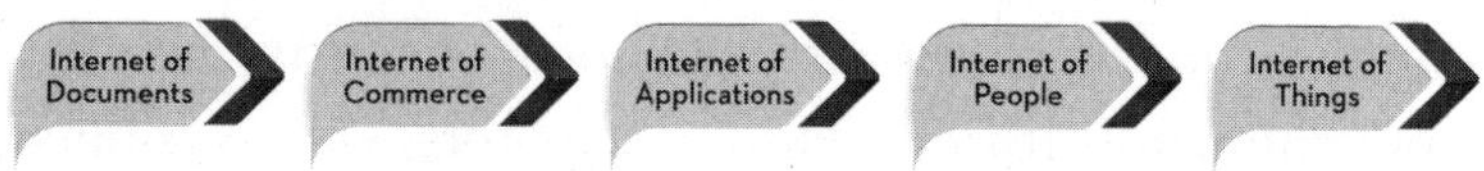

Effect of Internet of Things in Different Sectors

The key sectors that have been impacted by IoT are:

- Health
- Manufacturing
- Financial services
- Retail
- Farming

Health: Advancement of the health sector with the help of IoT will benefit not only the patients but would also ensure efficient functioning of the healthcare sector. IoT has eased the monitoring of patients by doctors. For instance, sensors fitted in the patients' body can monitor the health conditions of the patients as well as can alert the doctors during any medical emergency.

Manufacturing: Internet of Things is playing a huge role in advancing the manufacturing sector. With each passing day, the need of IoT is becoming evident in the manufacturing sector, and organisations are also realising that unless they implement IoT, it would become tougher for them to cope with the growing competition and to meet the customers' demands. For instance, sensors fitted in the manufacturing parts give the servicemen an idea about the present condition of the machines and whether a change/repair is required or not, thus preventing the organisation from potential damage of machinery.

Financial services: Internet of Things is in its initial stage in the banking and financial services sectors. It has huge potential to completely transform this sector. Banking and financial services sectors deal with a huge amount of data. IoT can benefit the financial services sector by performing functions, such as gathering, transferring and analysing data accurately.

Did You Know?

According to the 2015 Global Shopper Survey, 96% of retailers are ready to bring IoT devices into their operations in the hope that it will strengthen relationships with consumers.

Source: 'The Future of Retail Through the Internet of Things'. https://www.intel.com/content/dam/www/public/us/en/documents/white-papers/future-retail-through-iot-paper.pdf

Retail: The retail industry has always responded positively to technological changes to improve customer experiences and to satisfy them. IoT is making significant impact on the retail industry, not only by improving the shopping experience of the customers but also by making retailers much more profitable. IoT gives retailers far greater insight into who their customer is, how the products are performing, etc.

Farming: The farming industry would get more attention than ever before in the coming decades. The world would need to produce 70 per cent more food in 2050 than it did in 2006 in order to feed the growing population of the earth according to the UN Food and Agriculture Organisation. To meet this demand, farmers and agricultural companies are turning to the IoT for analytics and greater production capabilities. The benefits that farmers get from IoT application in agriculture are twofold. First, these systems help farmers decrease production costs and waste by optimising the use of inputs. Second, IoT can increase yields by improving its decision-making process with more accurate data.

Internet of Things: A Threat to Cyber Security

The Oxford English Dictionary defines the Internet of Things as a proposed development of the Internet in which everyday objects have network connectivity, allowing them to send and receive data. Now with this exchange of data comes security issues. Here, we will summarise the findings of the Open Web Application Security Project (OWASP) Internet of Things Top Ten Project that highlights the top ten security issues with IoT devices. The OWASP IoT Project is designed to facilitate a better understanding of IoT security issues by manufacturers, developers and users, and to enable them to make better security decisions related to IoT technologies. The security issues are:

- Insecure web interface
- Insufficient authentication/authorisation

- Insecure network services
- Lack of transport encryption
- Privacy concerns
- Insecure cloud interface
- Insecure mobile interface
- Insecure security configurability
- Insecure software/firmware
- Poor physical security

Insecure web interface: Web interfaces allows a user to get access to the IoT device and interact with it. But at the same time, web interfaces could allow an attacker to gain unauthorised access to the device due to the vulnerabilities like weak default credentials, credentials exposed in network traffic, session management, weak account lockout settings, etc.

Insufficient authentication/authorisation: This area deals with ineffective and poor authorisation mechanism through which the user accesses the IoT devices. Vulnerabilities, such as lack of password complexity, poorly protected credentials, lack of two-factor authentication, insecure password recovery, lack of role-based access control and absence of the option to change the username and password.

Insecure network services: This point deals with the vulnerabilities of the network services that are used to access the IoT devices. Insecure network services might allow an intruder to gain unauthorised access to the IoT devices or to the data associated with it. Vulnerabilities that are responsible for this issue include: vulnerable services, buffer overflow, open ports via UPnP (Universal Plug and

Play), exploitable UDP (User Datagram Protocol) services and denial of services.

Lack of transport encryption: When the data is exchanged between the IoT devices in an unencrypted format, then it becomes easier for hackers to get access to that data. Vulnerabilities, such as unencrypted services via the Internet, unencrypted services via the local network, poorly implemented SSL (Secure Sockets Layer)/TLS (Transport Layer Security), misconfigured SSL/TLS and absence of firewall option can lead to this issue.

Privacy concerns: Privacy concerns arise when organisations collect a lot of data but are unable to provide adequate security to safeguard those data. Collecting more sensitive data or unnecessary data is the main reason for this concern.

Insecure cloud interface: It is concerned with the security issues related to the cloud interface used to interact with the IoT devices. Poor authentication and transferring data in an unencrypted format are the reasons which allow the attackers to access the device or the data. Security vulnerabilities that could lead to this problem are account enumeration, no account lockout, credentials exposed to network traffic, etc.

Insecure mobile interface: Similar to the previous point, weak authentication and unencrypted data transfer are the reasons for this issue.

Insecure security configurability: Non-availability of password option at the IoT devices, transferring data in the unencrypted medium, insecure logging and absence of alerts and notifications for security events are the reasons behind this issue.

Insecure software/firmware: Whenever there is non-availability of updates in the existing software/firmware, it becomes a security concern of its own. A software becomes vulnerable when the updated files are not encrypted or when the files are transmitted without encryption. Securing the update servers is also a way to avoid the security concern.

Poor physical security: Physical external ports, such as USB ports, increase the security risks of IoT devices. Accessing the devices through external ports may put in malware or viruses thus making the device vulnerable. Furthermore, external ports may be used to access the configuration of the device, ultimately leading to unauthorised access of the device or the data.

In addition to the above-mentioned threats, IoT technology poses certain other vulnerabilities. They are as follows:

Limited resources: Most of the IoT devices have restricted capabilities when it comes to processing and memory. This hampers their ability to effectively incorporate advance security features.

Complex ecosystem: Because of the high security risks, the IoT cannot be considered as merely a system of independent devices. Rather, it has now become a complex arrangement of diverse devices, communication interfaces and people.

Low cost: In certain cases, manufacturers limit the security features in order to provide the device at a lower cost. Such measures lead to reduced efficacy of the product's security features and thereby offer less protection against certain types of IoT attacks.

Lack of experience: IoT cyber security is still in its nascent stage. Even though it has developed in the past few years, there is lack of expertise in this field to understand mistakes committed earlier, rectify them and put them to practice. Though there are general rules to be followed, it does not compensate for the skills and experience of IoT experts.

Security failures in the device's design and its exploitation: In their bid to launch products faster than their competitors, manufacturers sometimes neglect the need to develop essential cyber-security features such as end-to-end encryption of transmitted information.

Lack of control and asymmetry of the information: More often than not, users are not aware of how their data is being treated by devices with sensorisation technology. Such information is not provided to them at the time of obtaining their consent. This information asymmetry results in users losing control of the treatment of their personal data as in most cases, this information is shared with third parties without their consent. Though not specific to IoT, lack of information control in cloud and big data services has the potential to spill over to IoT.

Limitations in the possibility of maintaining anonymity when using services: An important feature offered by cyberspace is that it allows a user to be anonymous. However, with the advancement in IoT, there are chances of losing this anonymity for using various services. To preserve anonymity, it is necessary to improve encryption and access control techniques. Further, new techniques need to be developed which support the concept of privacy by design, avoid interference of information and also maintain the privacy of the user's location.

Security against efficiency: Manufacturers face many challenges in their bid to optimise the device's hardware with the required security features. One of them is time constraint. The pressure to commercialise an IoT product is relatively more compared to other fields. This sometimes leads to compromises with the security of the device. Another issue is budget limitations. Both these issues, combined together, compel the companies to make IoT products focus more on the functionality and usability of the device rather than security.

Unclear responsibilities: When it comes to handling security issues, there is a lack of clear demarcation of responsibilities among the manufacturer, service provider and user. In addition to this, the manner of handling a security issue when a single component is shared by various parties is also obscure. This leads to ambiguity in case of a security threat. This is especially true for the large and complex IoT supply chain.

Measures to Be Taken to Tackle These Threats

Discussed below are the fundamental IoT security guidance as provided by OWASP.

Insecure web interface

- Weak passwords must be disallowed.
- The web interface of your IoT device must have an account lockout mechanism.
- The web interface in your IoT product must be tested for XSS (cross-site scripting), SQL (structured query language) and CSRF (cross-site request forgery) vulnerabilities.
- You must ensure that your IoT device has the ability to establish secure connections using https.
- The web interfaces of your IoT devices must be protected using web-application firewalls.
- You must ensure that the web interface of your IoT hardware permits you to change the default username and password.

Insufficient authentication/authorisation

- Make sure that any access-requiring authentication requires strong passwords.
- User roles should be properly segregated in multi-user environments.
- Two-factor authentication must be implemented wherever possible.
- Password-recovery mechanisms must be secure.
- Users should have the option to require strong passwords.
- Users must have the option to force password expiration after a specific period of time.
- Make sure that users have the option to change the default username and password.

Insecure network services

- You must ensure that all your IoT devices operate with a minimal number of active network ports.
- All your IoT devices should not make network ports.
- You must ensure that all devices do not make services available to the Internet via UPnP, for example.
- You should monitor all required network services for vulnerabilities such as buffer overflows or denial of service.

Lack of transport encryption

- You must ensure that all communication between system components as well as the traffic between the IoT devices and the Internet are encrypted.
- It is best to avoid proprietary protocols and instead use recommended and accepted encryption practices.
- You must ensure that protocols like SSL/TLS are implemented, updated and properly configured.
- You should consider making a firewall option available for the product.

Privacy concerns

- It must be ensured that a minimal amount of personal information is collected from the customers.
- All collected personal data of the customers must be protected using encryption.
- Only authorised individuals should have access to collect personal information.
- It must be ensured that only less sensitive data is collected.
- Make sure data is de-identified or anonymous.

Insecure cloud interface

- All cloud interfaces must be reviewed for security vulnerabilities.
- Cloud-based web interfaces should disallow weak passwords.
- Cloud-based web interfaces must have account lockout mechanism.
- Two-factor or multi-factor authentication must be implemented.
- Users must have the option to change the default username and password.

Insecure mobile interface

- Mobile applications should disallow weak passwords.
- Mobile applications must have account lockout mechanisms.
- Two or multi-factor authentication for mobile applications should be implemented.
- Make sure that any mobile application uses transport encryption.
- Users must have the option to force password expiration after a specific period of time.
- Users must have the option to change the default username and password.

Insufficient security configurability

- You must ensure that password security options are available.
- Encryption options must be available.
- Secure logging feature must be available.

- Make sure that alerts and notifications are available to the user for security events.

Insecure software/firmware

- Make sure all system devices have updation capability and can be updated quickly when vulnerabilities are discovered.
- Update files should be encrypted and the files should be transmitted using encryption.
- Update files must be signed and then validated by the device before installing.
- You must ensure that update servers are secure.
- The product must have the ability to implement scheduled updates.

Poor physical security

> *India has no cyber-security watchdog agency and the matter has become an issue that needs serious attention.*

- Make sure the device is produced with a minimal number of physical external ports (for example, USB ports).
- You must ensure that the firmware of the operating system cannot be accessed via unintended methods such as through an unnecessary USB port.
- The product should be tamper-resistant.
- The product must have the ability to limit administrative capability in some manner, possibly by only connecting locally for administrative function.
- The product must have the ability to disable external ports such as USB.

Internet of Things and Cyber Security: The Indian Perspective

India, the fastest-growing economy in the world, is spending a lot on IoT. More and more people are getting involved in IoT. According to the consultancy firm Deloitte, India's IoT market size is expected to reach $9 billion by 2020. With this growing number of IoT devices, cyber threats and breaches are becoming prominent day by day and taking into consideration the fact that India has no cyber-security watchdog agency, the matter has become an issue that needs some serious attention.

Internet of Things Hacking Incidents

Let us take a look at some of the major IoT hacking incidents over the past few years.

Mirai Botnet (Dyn Attack)

The attack took place in October 2016. It was the largest distributed DoS attack on service provider Dyn using an IoT botnet. The attack caused serious effect on major sites like Amazon.com, Netflix, Visa, Pinterest, Twitter, Reddit, Paypal, Starbucks, etc.

Things to learn from the Mirai Botnet attack:

- Never implement IoT devices which do not have their software, passwords or firmware updated.
- At the time of installation of any new device to your IT network, you must remember to change the default username and password.
- Every IoT device must have a different and unique password. Refrain from using the same password for all your IoT devices.

- In order to protect your IoT devices against cyber threats, they must always be patched with the latest software and firmware updates.

The TRENDnet Webcam Hack

TRENDnet is a global computer networking manufacturer company, headquartered at Torrance, California, US. The company marketed its SecurView cameras for various uses like home security, baby monitoring, etc. Though the company claimed that its products were safe, it was later discovered that these cameras were faulty and anyone who obtained the IP address of the products could easily access it and look through it and in some cases even listen through it.

St Jude Medical Hack

In early 2017, it was revealed by the US Food and Drug Administration that pacemakers of St Jude Medical, an American global medical device company headquartered in Minnesota, US, possessed certain vulnerabilities that could potentially enable hackers to access the device and subsequently control the pacemaker remotely. Through this remote-control mechanism, hackers could deplete the battery-life of the pacemaker, alter programmed settings or change the beats and rhythm of the pacemaker so as to administer incorrect pacing or shocks to patients. As soon as the vulnerabilities were detected, heart patients with St Jude's pacemakers were urged to update their firmware. Although no patients were harmed, the entire incident was a risky affair!

The Internet of Things and Cyber Security: What You Need to Know

The Internet of Things is proving revolutionary in how we engage with technology. These days, everything is connected to the Internet—from fridges and smart televisions at home to security cameras and even cars at work. Even light bulbs are now controllable through an application on your phone and your wireless connection.

The benefits of the IoT are significant. Through the IoT, we gain great control over our technology environment. Whether we are able to use it to save money, in terms of cutting power bills by remotely accessing air conditioners, lights and so on, or in helping to keep our office secure by watching security camera feeds from anywhere, the IoT takes the already ubiquitous technology that we all live with, to the next level; it makes technology a seamless part of our day-to-day lives.

But, there are serious security considerations and risks that we need to be aware of as well. A study found that more often than not, IoT devices have serious security vulnerabilities. In fact, a full 70 per cent of IoT devices are easy to hack, and this is something that we need to talk about because with people using IoT devices for everything, this means there are serious potential risks that people need to be prepared for.

How Do I Protect Myself Without Giving Up My Internet of Things Technology?

To save your IoT from becoming botnets in the hands of cybercriminals, you do not need to give up your IoT technology altogether! All you need to do in order to be safe from cyber threats is use your IoT devices in a responsible manner. Adopt and follow best practices in IoT cyber security, adhere to them and you will have significantly reduced the risk of your IoT devices being affected by various cyberattacks. There are certain baseline measures you could adopt to ensure the safety of your IoT technology:

Maintain a strong password hygiene

It is advisable that you use strong and unique passwords across all your IoT devices. Avoid using easily hackable passwords, such as 'admin' as a username and 'password' as the password. This is a very common mistake that most users make. Also, make sure that while setting up your IoT hardware, you do not miss changing the default username and password. Sometimes an IoT device may not have a username/password feature. It is best to avoid such devices.

Disable remote access to devices

To avoid cyberattacks, you should strongly consider disabling remote access to your IoT devices. Also, when you are connected to the Internet, make sure that a secure connection has been established via protocol ports like SSH (Secure Shell) and https. These protocols not only encrypt all communication between your browser and the websites that you visit, but also block unauthorised access by external parties, such as hackers. It is possible that you will want to enable remote access services on some of your IoT devices; in that case, you must consider using stringent security measures on such devices. Also, disable remote access on devices that do not necessarily require it.

> *Buy your IoT devices from reputable organisations that have trustworthy records in providing devices with cyber-security measures.*

Buy devices from reputable organisations

When purchasing IoT devices, make sure you buy them from reputable organisations that have trustworthy records in providing devices with cyber-security measures. It is imperative that you keep your IoT devices updated and patched in order to avoid being vulnerable to cyber threats. Also, refrain from buying IoT devices that don't have regular software updates. Further, when a vendor discontinues supporting a particular device, you must consider upgrading to its latest available version that supports regular security updates.

Train your staff

It is of utmost importance that your IT team is adequately trained about IoT security measures, which enables them to effectively deploy and safely add additional technology on to your IT network. Further, employees other than in your IT department must also be trained on IoT security. For instance, it is possible that the physical security team of your organisation may want to install IoT enabled security cameras to watch the building remotely. In such a scenario, your physical security team members must be taught the proper manner of installing such cameras onto your existing IT network so that they are cyber-secure.

Never assume you are safe

The best possible way to prevent a cyberattack is to never assume that you are safe from cyber-security threats. You must adopt and implement the best security practices for your IoT devices, and must always be on the lookout for any aberrant behaviour exhibited by your IoT hardware. For instance, IoT devices, in general, 'call back' and 'talk' to only the manufacturer's server. Therefore, if you see any or all of your IoT devices connecting to other servers, it is proof of a cyber intrusion. Thus, implementing security measures alone is not enough; you should also monitor the activity of your devices to detect any compromised device.

Cyber Security for the Internet of Things: Solutions

Let us now look into some cyber-security solutions pertaining to IoT devices. An effective cyber-security solution for Internet of Things must, at minimum, consist of the following measures:

- Data on the IoT devices must be secured with key management and encryption.
- An IoT device must be equipped with sensors that are able to detect anomalies in sensor data.
- Strong encryption must be maintained where data is aggregated as well as at the edge where it is collected.
- IoT devices must be monitored to detect abnormal behaviour, which could be indicative of a cyber intrusion.
- A dashboard should be created using data science and machine learning that shows potential cyber threats.

Now that we have understood about the intersection of cyber security with IoT, it is time to explore another exciting and upcoming area in the field of cyber security, that is, artificial intelligence (AI). The following chapter discusses the role of AI in cyber security.

6

CYBER SECURITY AND ARTIFICIAL INTELLIGENCE

In the previous chapters, we have understood the importance of cyber security. Now, it's time to wonder how to make the whole system of cyber security more efficient. As malware attacks have increased both in volume and complexity, it has become very difficult for the traditional model of analytics to keep up with the load. This marks the need for the introduction of other means which would make the process of analytics much more cost-effective and efficient.

Introduction to Various Forms of Analytics in Cyber Security

For data analytics, three concepts are often used interchangeably but each of them has its own unique relevance. The three concepts are:

- Artificial intelligence (AI)
- Machine learning
- Data science

Figure 6.1 What is Artificial Intelligence?

> *The traditional modes of analytics have become redundant.*

Artificial intelligence (AI) is a very broad concept and in simple terms it can be described as a process which makes the machines mimic humans by imparting basic functions, such as understanding, sensing and responding. AI needs two things in order to mimic human behaviour—knowledge and action.

Machine learning is a subset of AI and it involves learning from past data and subsequently creating a knowledge base from information derived from such data. This is an important aspect of machine learning as it codifies the rules which human experts know. This is how they build knowledge.

Did You Know?

Machine learning is essentially learning from data. Data is the key ingredient for machine learning. Machine learning can only be as good as the data you use to train it.

Source: 'Differences Between AI and Machine Learning, and Why it Matters'. https://medium.com/datadriveninvestor/differences-between-ai-and-machine-learning-and-why-it-matters-1255b182fc6

Machine learning may be categorised into:

- Supervised machine learning
- Unsupervised machine learning

The difference between supervised and unsupervised machine learning can be explained using fruits. Let us imagine that we are given different fruits and we are given a task to arrange them in separate baskets. So, in this current scenario, suppose the fruits which are given to us are apples, oranges, bananas and cherries. Here, we already know from our previous knowledge which fruit is what according to its shape and hence we can sort out and arrange them in a particular order. This will work as you'll have an image of a particular fruit in mind and if anything is similar to that image, you shall quickly place it under that category. This is an example of supervised machine learning where you have already learnt the things you have to do, so the job is done in a confident manner.

Figure 6.2 Categories of Machine Learning

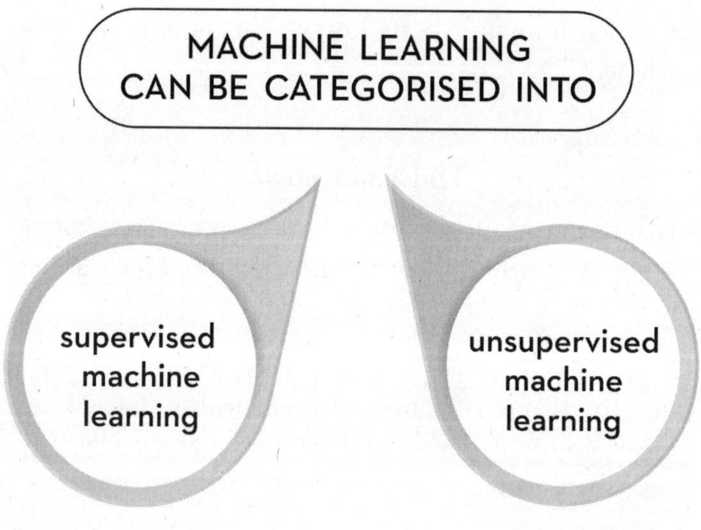

Supervised learning steps

- The data has been provided to the system that contains the pictures of fruits and it has been informed which picture is classified as which fruit.
- The aforementioned process is called labelling and for supervised machine learning, labelling is necessary.
- The model learns from the labelled data and it can easily identify the fruits.

In another scenario, consider you have to sort the fruits and arrange them, but in this case, you do not have prior knowledge of the fruits. This raises the problem of sorting fruits and arranging them in order. In this scenario, you will take a few characteristics into consideration and you will use that to sort different fruits. This will be done by taking characteristics such as colour, size and so on. Using these characteristics, we can sort out the fruits by attributing the characteristics to different fruits. This is what unsupervised machine learning looks like. This can be used to reduce the number of dimensions or field and can group records together.

Unsupervised learning steps

- In this method, the system is provided with pictures of different kinds of fruits and is asked to separate and categorise them. In this case, unlike the previous one, no labelling is done.
- Since there is no availability of labelled fruits, the system will look for various patterns in the fruits such as their shape, size, colour and shall assign these

attributes to different fruits. The same attributes will help it segregate and categorise the fruits.

To sum up, the differences between supervised and unsupervised learning are as follows:

- **Types of data:** In the case of supervised machine learning, the type of data is labelled and in case of unsupervised it is unlabelled.
- **Feedback:** In the case of supervised machine learning, the system learns from the output and keeps it in mind while in the case of unsupervised learning, there is no feedback involved.
- **Function:** Supervised learning is used to predict data; on the other hand, the task of unsupervised learning is to find structures in data.

Data science is nothing but defined data sets which assist machine learning by providing data collection, preparation and integration. To make machine-learning work, data science comes into play.

But the question which now arises is: How is AI or machine learning helpful in maintaining cyber security? To answer this question, we need to understand our goal of applying machine learning to cyber security. To explain the goal in a broad statement we can say that machine learning helps in finding anomalies. Machine

Data science is nothing but defined data sets which assist machine learning by providing data collection, preparation and integration.

learning helps us to identify malware and unwanted behaviour.

It's like asking a child to sort out mangoes and bananas from a pile and put them in separate baskets. We can teach the child the difference between the fruits and the child can use his cognitive skills to sort out the piles and report anomalies if there are any.

AI helps in overcoming the two barriers of cyber security—huge amount of data and multiple languages.

Data

The amount of data produced every day globally is beyond human control and imagination. In the past 10 years, a huge amount of data has posed a threat to cyber security but thanks to AI, this problem can be dealt with now. To understand the volume of data we are talking about, let us have a look at a few figures. In the year 2017, the statistics of data generated per minute comprised:

- 4,55,000 tweets
- 5,10,000 comments and 2,93,000 statuses on Facebook
- 400 hours of videos on YouTube
- 36,07,080 searches on Google
- 18,60,00,000 sent emails

If we combine these figures with alerts, which organisations receive from user activity and other related activities, it becomes evident that it is beyond the capability of humans to analyse this data in isolation. This is where AI comes in!

It has been a long-held principle that the key to security is to balance out the time and context. The threats should be dealt with immediately, and an important task, which should not be missed, is to understand the nature of the threats.

Machines can help in this process by analysing massive volumes of data at a fraction of the time taken by humans to complete the same task. Machine learning may not be able to take actions by itself, but it can help in the processing of data and can provide a detailed analysis.

Multiple Languages

Another barrier for creating actionable intelligence is the language barrier. Majority of the information required by security professionals is buried in unstructured text. This problem can be solved with the help of natural language processing (NLP). It enables machines to collect data and make sense of it irrespective of the language, format or even punctuation. An effective and powerful NLP can even understand jargon and slang across all languages. This is something which is beyond the imagination of security analysts.

Did You Know?

NLP research is thriving as it can be used for any written text. Data scientists at Endgame are applying NLP to identify malicious code by using NLP for malware analysis. This is being done by automating the identification of malicious code masquerading as a benign code.

Source: 'NLP For Security: Malicious Language Processing'. https://www.endgame.com/blog/technical-blog/nlp-security-malicious-language-processing

Applications of Artificial Intelligence in Cyber-security Operations

Although there is no fixed form or limit to the applications of AI, a few examples of how AI can be used in cyber security are mentioned in Figure 6.3 below.

> *An effective and powerful NLP can even understand the jargon and the slang across all languages.*

Figure 6.3 Application of AI in Cyber Security

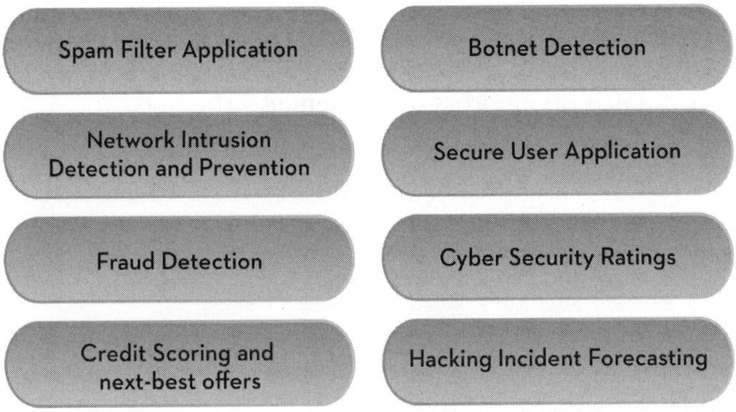

Did You Know?

The scientists at CERN (the European Organisation for Nuclear Research) have decided to skip the standard cyber-security measures and rely on AI for protection of their massive network of computers, which help them unravel the mystery of the universe. They are teaching their AI to distinguish between usual and unusual activity so that they can act when needed.

Source: 'An Advanced AI Has Been Deployed to Fight Against Hackers'. https://futurism.com/an-advanced-ai-has-been-deployed-to-fight-against-hackers

Need for AI in Cyber Security

The world has never seen more varied forms of cyber threats as it is seeing today. The attacks have been getting more sophisticated, regular and impactful. There is an urgent need to use advance tools and technologies to get one step ahead of such threats. At the same time, there is a critical shortage of security professionals.

> *Hyper-connected workplaces and their dependence on cloud systems demand the need for AI in cyber security.*

Moreover, hyper-connected workplaces and their dependence on cloud systems demand the need for AI in cyber security. Businesses have been depending on IoT and to make it more reliable, businesses need to investigate new technologies to protect the end users and broaden their customer base.

Reduce human efforts

One of the major reasons for automation is to reduce human efforts as around one-third of the time is spent in gathering and processing information which can be automated. One such example of automation is IBM's Watson supercomputer which investigates 4 million security-related documents in just one hour.

> *IBM's Watson supercomputer investigates 4 million security-related documents in just one hour!*

How is the work done by AI better than humans?

> *The purpose of AI is to perform an activity in much lesser time than that of an expert human mind.*

AI involves creating a decision-making mechanism, which is similar to the decision-making mechanism of the human brain. The purpose of AI is to do something which an expert human mind can do, but in much lesser time. This is helpful in cases where there is a huge amount of data to be analysed by an expert in a given time; AI in these situations can come up with fast and successful solutions.

For example, in case of diagnosis of a disease, the process which the doctor follows in detecting the disease can be modelled with artificial intelligence. This would result in AI diagnosing it in the same way a doctor would, and it can be used where there is no available expert in that field. This can only work if data, which is appropriate and related to the problem, is collected.

Did You Know?

IBM Watson is a service that runs on 90 servers with 2,880 processor cores running concurrently. It has 16TB of RAM. The core function is related to IBM's DeepQA technology, which is a question and answer system. Using this system, a human can ask a question and Watson shall direct and answer the question.

Source: 'This is Watson'. https://ieeexplore.ieee.org/xpl/tocresult.jsp?isnumber=6177717

How is it different from traditional methods?

Helps meet the increased demand for workforce

> *It has been estimated that there will be around 3.5 million unfilled cyber-security positions worldwide.*

Cyber security, using AI and machine learning, has made it easier to respond to security threats. The scariest truth about the increase in cyber threats is that most businesses, and the cyber-security industry itself, are not very well prepared to tackle them. The prime reason for this is that due to the increase in this demand for services, the workforce has been having a very hard time meeting it. The positions available currently will be increased several times in the coming years. It has been estimated that there will be around 3.5 million unfilled cyber-security positions worldwide. To compensate for this demand, the current workforce must either work hard or they have to work for longer hours. This has made it tough for the workforce to respond to threats appropriately and effectively. This problem can be addressed by AI. There is an urgent need to implement AI in cyber security as circumstances demand it.

Assists experts and adapts over time

AI, with the help of newer algorithms, has made detection of new-generation malware very easy—something which was not detectable using conventional methods. The new-generation machine learning can adapt over time and has a more dynamic approach than conventional methods. The solutions provided by machine learning rely on data which has been obtained from prior cyberattacks and can prepare the system to respond to newer but similar risks. AI can help assign red flags to threats or anomalous activities by studying and learning from prior data, which cannot be done by humans due to lack of time and resources. With this method, AI will not render the experts useless but will assist them to tackle the threats efficiently and effectively. The security methods can use artificial intelligence to use the existing data to handle malware and attacks of the new generation.

The Role of AI in Encryption

What is encryption?

Encryption is the translation of data into secret codes and is the most effective way of achieving data security. To open an encrypted file, one must have access to the key or password, which will decrypt the file to make it readable again. The unencrypted data is called 'plain text' and the encrypted one is called 'cipher text'. The basic form of encryption is replacing every alphabet with an alternate one, for example, the encrypted word for APPLE can be BQQMF.

> *What Is Encryption?*
>
> *Encryption is the translation of data into secret codes and is the most effective way to achieve cyber security.*

Current use of AI in encryption

Although the current use of AI in encryption is very limited and not at par with human-generated encryption, it is anticipated that in the future, AI will be able to rewrite encryption keys and do it repeatedly so that it can avoid getting unlocked by hackers outside the organisation.

An Instance of Use of AI in Encryption

Recently, Google was successful in teaching the neural network as to how to encrypt and decrypt messages. There were three neural networks called Alice, Bob and Eve which were created. Each of the networks was assigned its own job, which was to send the secret message and to decrypt it; one was given the task of deciphering the message without actually possessing the secret key. The result was that after 15,000 simulations, the two neural networks were able to send and decrypt messages in a secured way and Eve, whose task was to decrypt the message, couldn't do it.

After this research was carried out, it was concluded that neural networks could be trained to protect certain information and also protect from attacks. The research also stated that it may be improbable that the neural network would become great at cryptanalysis (art of deciphering without having the key), but it may prove itself to be useful in making sense of metadata and traffic analysis.

Possible application

According to the 2018 Annual Cybersecurity Report of Cisco (a world-renowned IT and networking company), malware is often hidden within encrypted web traffic and transmitted through cloud systems. This makes the need for putting in adequate tools to prevent the use of encryption for masking malicious activities. The report further suggests that AI could be taught to detect unusual patterns in encrypted web traffic and could help in improving security defences. In this way, AI could also help in monitoring encrypted networks.

The Role of AI in Overcoming the Skill Gap

Did You Know?

There is a huge difference in supply and demand for cyber-security positions. Currently, there are 3.5 lakh unfilled cyber-security positions in the US and it has been predicted that by the year 2021, the global shortfall will reach 3.5 million. This problem has arisen due to lack of investment in education, market misalignment and bad marketing.

Source: 'Cybersecurity Supply/Demand Heat Map'. https://www.cyberseek.org/heatmap.html

Reasons for 'the skill gap' are:

- Difficulties in hiring because new employees may not be adequately trained or educated to deal with complex and difficult cyber-security issues.
- Companies may not be sure as to what to look for in an employee as cyber security is a diverse and dynamic field and various skills are needed which are subject to change.
- Even after the employees are hired, they are often overworked as they must be aware of all the developments in their respective fields.

Did You Know?

In 2019, the demand for cyber-security talent is expected to rise to 6 million globally, with a projected shortfall of 1.5 million. As per NASSCOM, India alone will need 1 million cyber-security professionals by 2020 to meet the rising demands of its rapidly growing economy.

Source: 'Cybersecurity Jobs Report'. https://www.herjavecgroup.com/wp-content/uploads/2018/07/HG-and-CV-The-Cybersecurity-Jobs-Report-2017.pdf

Can Automation Bridge the Skill Gap?

Since it has been mentioned that one of the major reasons for using AI in cyber security is to meet the shortage in workforce, hence, automation can bridge the gap. It has been highlighted that there already exists a shortage of cyber-security personnel and in future, the shortage may increase. The question which now arises is: Can the automation bridge the gap completely by itself? The answer to this question is 'no'. To understand the answer, we need to consider the steps that a cyber-security analyst must take through the entire lifecycle of a cyber-security incident. The following are the steps involved:

- **Preparation**: It involves having a workable plan in case an incident occurs; this is like conducting drills and ensuring that apt mitigation steps are taken in case a situation arises.
- **Prevention**: Even though it is impossible to stop all attacks, steps should be taken to prevent a successful one. This involves researching on potential threats and finding vulnerabilities.

- **Detection**: To address an attack, it must be first detected. All incidents which raise an alarm are not necessarily a threat. So, it is upon the organisation to determine and distinguish between a genuine attack and a false alarm.
- **Containment**: Once the attack is detected and analysis shows that it is a genuine attack, the damage that occurs has to be contained. The longer the malware stays in the system, the more damage it will cause.
- **Eradication**: If malware has managed to infect computers then it must be removed from all of them.
- **Recovery**: After the attack has occurred, it is very important for business to get back on its usual course. For example, after a ransomware attack, it is important to recover by scrubbing all hard drives and restoring from a clean backup.
- **Forensics**: After the incident has occurred, it is important to conduct a postmortem which involves analysing the breach to avoid similar attacks in future.

Incorporating humans with automation

The skill gap issue can be addressed with the help of collaborative, investigative methods with the help of automation. In the present scenario, automation can help but it cannot handle every task. It can reduce workload by filtering false alarms and providing periodic updates to assign tasks to specific analysts. Incorporating humans with automation is the perfect combination for defending against cyberattacks. This might not address the skills problem completely but reduces the problem to a certain extent.

The issue of skill gap can be addressed by collaborative and investigative methods with the help of automation.

This can be made possible in the following scenarios:

- Where hunting for attacks is a hit-or-miss proposition that can be extremely time-consuming, AI can be the saviour there and can help in identifying the potential threats and unusual patterns. This will help in eradicating the threats.
- Machine learning can also help junior analysts as it can learn how to respond to different threats in the same way as experts do, and it can also recommend these actions to junior analysts. It can also identify people who are experts in that problem and approach them directly.

Did You Know?

Organisations can waste as much as $1.3 million per year responding to 'inaccurate and erroneous intelligence' or 'chasing erroneous alerts'.

Source: 'Artificial Intelligence for Cybersecurity'. https://www.aiaa.org/protocolAI/

Current Operation of AI in Cyber Security by Companies

The field of cyber security is seeing a shift towards context-aware behavioural analytics which will help in identifying suspicious behaviour or transactions. A very simple example of this is how we get a notification every time a login attempt is made on a different device or in an unfamiliar location. Companies are becoming extremely aggressive with respect to cyber security and have been making attempts to prevent and track these attacks to the greatest extent. It has been estimated that expenditure on cyber security is going to increase rapidly by the year 2022 and that most of this investment shall be made into AI and machine learning as the human factor is a weak link in cyber security. These new technologies have been predicted to lessen human intervention and shall rely more on the incorporation of machines. It has also been expected that these new changes will be customisable and will not be one-size-fits-all.

Let us now look at some companies and their AI assistants.

Companies and Their AI Assistants

IBM's Watson

IBM's Watson was made keeping in mind that AI is the future of cyber security and it was made to detect threats faster. It uses cognitive technology to fend off hackers and addresses two main challenges which are—manual checking of online content, which requires hours due to the shortage of cyber-security analysts. With IBM's Watson, the cyber-security analysts can delegate the tedious and time-consuming job of threat research to AI. It helps the analysts to sort through huge volumes of data at a speed which is much more than that of a human. It also addresses the threats which go unnoticed by manual investigations. IBM's QRadar with Watson augments the ability of analysts to understand threats by relating it to local security threats.

McAfee

McAfee has decided to forge ahead with innovative methods such as analytics, deep learning and AI. The main aim of this move was to enable the security team to discover and deal with the threats, and rule out the threats completely. This was initiated as the security teams were completely overwhelmed by the complexities of attacks.

The technology developed by McAfee reconstructs the cyberattacks that have happened in the past and builds tools and platforms using data science methodology. By doing this, it helps in bringing machine learning and humans together to deal with and tackle the security issues and thereby stopping the attacks.

Darktrace—Enterprise Immune System

The Enterprise Immune System is one of the world's most advanced cyber-security systems, which involves machine learning for cyber defence. It is inspired by the self-learning system of the human immune system and has paved a way for an entirely new method of cyber security used by companies which have been facing threats in the current era where they are becoming advanced and sophisticated.

This method is inspired by the human immune system which is very complex and involves adaption to new forms of threats. It functions by learning what is normal in the body and identifies the problems that do not fit the normal pattern. A similar logic has been applied by Darktrace as it uses machine learning and Artificial Intelligence to learn about every device and user on a network to develop an insight as to what is normal and uses these insights to understand the emerging threats which might otherwise go unnoticed.

Like the human immune system, the enterprise immune system does not require a previous existence of threat and works automatically by using the insights to understand and tackle the threat in real time. It does not require any prior knowledge to understand whether an activity is potentially threatening or not.

Cylance
This start-up has created artificial intelligence, which uses machine learning to build services that replicate human thinking to solve more complex problems that can be solved by the human brain. This AI has been trained to think like a hacker. It works by predicting how malware can potentially attack networks and, in turn, helps the engineers to develop expertise in dealing with all new cyberattacks. Through this, the company believes that there are various benefits attached to it, especially the three S's—simple, seamless, silent. The organisations can thus have protection against cyberattacks by using fewer resources and reducing the cost to a significant margin. It helps in predicting malware and integrates into systems.

The Role of AI in Cyber Security: Boon or Bane?

With the emergence of AI and the level of automation brought by it, the next question which arises is: Whether AI and cyber security will be a partnership that both cyber security and cyber-criminals put their faith in? In other words, AI in cyber security is a double-edged sword—just as it can enhance and improve cyber-security measures, it can also multiply cyber threats when used by cyberattackers. Therefore, is AI in cyber security a boon or a bane? This can be better understood after exploring the risks and opportunities associated with AI in cyber security.

Opportunities for AI in cyber security

Despite adopting cyber-security measures, companies still fall prey to cyberattacks mostly because such measures are unable to keep up with the ever-evolving cyber-threat landscape, massive data breaches and global cyber-warfare, the speed and magnitude of which are increasing multifold. This is where AI can intervene and lend a helping hand. Let us read about the various ways in which AI can benefit the cyber-security system.

- **AI can help detect anomalies, malware and other cyberattack vectors automatically and in real time**. This not only reduces the incidence of cyber-security crimes, but also speeds up the time taken to detect cyber intrusions, thus enabling cyber-security analysts to focus on developing more efficient methods of cyber protection.
- **AI could anticipate future cyberattacks by using predictive analytics**. This is achieved by establishing cyber-threat models taken from continuously changing data sources, such as links, networks, architecture protocols and the state of network nodes. AI can interpret data from these sources to continuously identify present vulnerabilities and to, subsequently, counterattack and prevent any future attacks or threats.
- **Machine-learning-based software can efficiently spot similarities between various cyberattacks** or threats, especially when such attacks are coordinated by other automation software. Newer AI-based algorithms can interpret data originating from various sources/tools and can efficiently spot critical correlations between such data, which can easily escape human eyes.

AI can help in fraud detection and emergency management.

- **AI can help in emergency management**. AI can be applied to disaster response, enabling quick and efficient management of emergency situations. AI, with the help of predictive analytics, can analyse and assess the extent of damage and risk in a given area, thus helping emergency response teams prioritise their interventions and provide help first to victims who need it the most. Further, AI can perform tasks like image recognition, data extrapolation and classification at a much higher speed by using incoming data and pictures from satellites or crowd-sourced mapping material. AI can process, analyse and interpret images from various social networking sites such as Facebook, Instagram and Twitter to filter real information from fake, and can even locate the whereabouts of missing people. Several AI systems, using speech-to-text and analytics programs, can be employed to listen to emergency calls, thereby easing off the burden of emergency contact centres during times of disaster or emergencies. AI not only helps in reducing call times but also helps emergency-response teams by providing them with accurate information and planning the quickest routes to the disaster location.
- **AI can help in detection of fraud**. Biometrics powered by AI can identify, measure and analyse not only physical and facial features, but also specific human behaviours. With the help of 'emotion-recognition' technology, AI can read human emotions through a combination of advanced image

and audio processing. The AI-powered emotion-recognition software can capture and interpret facial expressions intertwined with mood, personality and human communication; it can even interpret micro-expressions to predict the actions of a human individual. Further, biometrics along with NLP (Natural Language Processing) and text analytics can analyse and interpret complex sentences and text and deduce the intentions behind such texts. A combination of all these systems and features can be utilised by law-enforcement agencies to detect information during interrogation, predict criminal behaviour, restrict dangerous situations and even fight terrorist activities.

Thus, in correct hands, AI can boost security measures to a huge extent. For instance, Barclays Africa is already using AI and machine learning to detect and respond to cyber-security threats. We can only assume that with time, most organisations may employ AI as a security measure. Let us now read about the risks brought about by AI in cyber security.

Risks of AI in cyber security

Before evaluating the risks posed by AI in cyber security, let us first explore a couple of instances that illustrate the manner in which AI is/can be weaponised to perpetrate cyber-security breaches.

Use of AI in Cyber Threats and Cyber Hacking

SNAP_R

In 2016, two data scientists, John Seymour and Philip Tully, from a social media security and digital risk-monitoring firm called ZeroFOX, performed a study on Twitter to determine who had a higher success rate of getting users to click on malicious links—humans or artificial intelligence, that is, who's better at phishing Twitter—humans or AI? Seymour and Tully developed an automated spear phishing tool known as SNAP_R (Social Media Automated Phishing and Reconnaissance), which used AI-powered LSTM (long short-term memory) algorithms. LSTM is capable of remembering long sequences of seemingly unstructured data, such as sentences, and was used to study tweets of a certain user, determine the most common topics they posted about and subsequently craft unique tweets that would interest the target. SNAP_R also employed machine learning to study the data revealed in various Twitter profiles such as bio-details or the number and kind of followers, and then form high-value target groups. The software would then pick a random minute during the hour in which a target is most likely to be active and send the synthesised tweet containing short URLs.

Results of the pilot experiment revealed that after sending 90 phishing posts to target users, there was a 17% clickthrough rate after two hours, and between 60–90% clickthrough rate after two days. It was observed in a man versus machine two-hour phishing contest that a human was able to generate phishing tweets by copy-pasting messages to different hashtags at the rate of 1.67 tweets per minute; whereas SNAP_R generated its phishing tweets at a rate of 6.85 tweets per minute! Further, SNAP_R could arbitrarily scale up its generation of phishing tweets with an increase in the number of machines. Also, in the two-hour contest, a human achieved 49 clickthroughs whereas SNAP_R achieved 275 clickthroughs, therefore proving that AI succeeded in getting users to click on malicious links.

In 2017, AI systems led to several automated and sophisticated social-engineering cyber hacking, with a first-of-its-kind malware emerging in early 2017 called 'smart malware' which is AI-powered and very difficult to detect.

Hacking inspired by DARPA (Defense Advanced Research Projects Agency) Cyber Grand Challenge

In 2016, a global hacking event was organised in Las Vegas—the DARPA-sponsored Cyber Grand Challenge—wherein seven competitors designed machines to cyber-hack other machines with the hope of winning $2 million as prize money. Each machine tried to find various ways to exploit software vulnerabilities and hack into others' systems and subsequently fix the damage caused by the cyber intrusions. The winning machine named Mayhem is kept in the Smithsonian National Museum of American History.

In 2017, a similar kind of artificial-intelligence technology was detected by the cyber-security firm, Darktrace, in a cyberattack that occurred in India. The malware employed AI to understand and analyse normal user behaviour patterns used in the network, mimic the behaviour of the network, systems and the users of the system, and then hide in the background, thus making it difficult to detect. Although the cyber intrusion was detected in its early stages of the attack, according to chief executive of Darktrace, Nicole Eagan, it was only the beginning of machine learning and artificial intelligence being used to attempt (and soon succeed at committing) cybercrimes.

Cyber-security researchers have identified multiple ways in which AI could be abused for perpetrating cybercrimes. Some of them are:

- **Cyber hacking would be made infinitely easier through the use of AI**. It would enable hackers to attack multiple targets at various places at a time or enable hacking in a much shorter amount of time. Further, with nations increasingly becoming electronically smart and digitised, and the increasing emergence of Internet of Things, AI could make virtually any device hackable, thus, effectively multiplying the effect of cyberattacks.
- **AI could make coding skills available to anyone**. This implies that cybercriminals could easily develop sophisticated malware efficient enough to circumvent security measures.
- **AI can be used to change narratives and distort reality by creating deceptive content**. Deepfake is an AI-powered software that can alter digital photographs and videos by replacing the face of one person with another. Similarly, Lyrebird3 can study and mimic short speech samples of a target individual via AI and create realistic-sounding speeches in the voice of the same individual.
- **AI coupled with machine learning can be used to automate cybercrimes**. Criminals can use AI and machine learning to create a communication process/ interaction between various tools and increase the incidence of, complicate or conceal cyberattacks. For instance, if one bot discovers a password, that bot can feed the information to a second bot, which can then be deployed to attack systems using the discovered password and so on.

- With AI, the **more common cybercrime techniques** such as botnet (where a network of software robots spread malicious software), zombie computers (hacking into a computer to launch cyberattacks), phishing, fast flux (where phishing websites can be made untraceable by quickly moving data) or skimmers (devices hacked to steal credit card information when a card is swiped), **would potentially multiply** not only in terms of number of attacks, but also in terms of severity of consequences and would become even more difficult to contain, mitigate or prevent.
- With **the level of automation** brought by AI, cyberattackers may recruit vast armies of machine-learning-powered bots or IoT botnets to deploy cyberattacks, thus **increasing the scale of their attacks drastically**. Further, AI-powered systems, with their newest algorithms, can generate 'smart malware' which can become much less detectable than regular malware, and labour-intensive attacks such as spear phishing can be performed with a much greater and improved efficiency when powered by AI.

> *AI can generate 'smart malware' which is extremely difficult to detect.*

It can thus be safely concluded that AI plays both the roles of a cop and a robber in cyber security. AI is a potent weapon in the hands of both a cyber-security professional as well as in the hands of a cybercriminal. Therefore, it must be kept in mind that only robots can beat robots. The only way to retaliate against AI-powered cyber threats is to employ AI-powered cyber-security mechanisms as well. Just as hackers are getting innovative, cyber-security analysts must also adopt adaptive and new revolutionary technologies brought about by AI and replace antiquated and obsolete systems of cyber security. Having understood the role of AI in cyber security, it is now time to discuss and determine if cloud computing has a similar relationship with cyber security in the next chapter!

7

CYBER SECURITY AND THE CLOUD

In the previous chapters, we learnt about cyber security, its management and its relationship with artificial intelligence. We are living in the 21st century and work confined to a place or office is not possible anymore. People carry their work along with them so it becomes pertinent that information should be stored in an accessible yet secure manner. This is where cloud computing saves the day.

To a person who is unaware of the developments in the technological space, the word 'cloud' would just be white fluffy things in the sky. For a software company, 'cloud' is the revolutionary advancement in the field of technology that has changed the face of storing and accessing data on applications and software. Until the inception of cloud computing, information was stored on a proprietary hard drive or local storage device, but cloud-based storage makes it possible to save them to a remote database. If an electronic device has access to the Internet, it has access to the data and the software programs to run it.

We are probably using cloud computing in our daily lives even if we are not aware of it. We use online services to send emails and edit documents; Hotstar or Netflix to watch our favourite TV series and movies; apps like Wynk, Saavn or Gaana to listen to music, etc., and for all these activities it is most likely that cloud computing is working in the background to store data. Cloud-computing services are relatively new to the software world, yet their usage is widespread. A variety of organisations from tiny start-ups to global corporations, government agencies, etc., are embracing the technology for their work.

Did You Know?

By the end of 2018, more than 30% of service-based companies migrated the larger part of their Enterprise Resource Planning (ERP) applications to the cloud environment.

Source: '2018 Trends In Cloud Computing'. https://www.comptia.org/resources/cloud-computing-trends-research

Cloud Computing: Meaning

Cloud computing is basically a method through which resources are recovered from the Internet through web-based tools and applications. It is called 'cloud computing' because the information is accessed in 'the cloud' and does not need the user to be in any specific location to access it. It helps the employees to work from any part of the world provided they have access to the Internet.

Did You Know?

In 2011, 90% of Microsoft's Research and Development budget was spent on cloud-computing strategy and products.

Source: 'Microsoft Steps Up R&D On Cloud Computing'. https://www.datacenterknowledge.com/archives/2011/04/19/microsoft-steps-up-rd-on-cloud-computing

Types of Cloud-computing Services

Before learning about the advantages and disadvantages of cloud computing over the traditional methods of storing data, it is important to know about the types of cloud computing that have evolved with time. Cloud computing is not a single piece of technology; like a microchip, it is a system which consists of three services:

- Infrastructure as a service (IaaS)
- Software as a service (SaaS)
- Platform as a service (PaaS)

Did You Know?

More and more companies are trying to get a foothold in China as part of their international expansion. The British Medical Journal (BMJ) is one among them which has worked with cloud services provider, Datapipe, to enter the Chinese market using Alibaba Cloud.

Source: 'Is Hyperconvergence Really Key to Your Data Centre Cloud Strategy?' https://www.cloudcomputing-news.net/news/2017/oct/16/hyperconvergence-really-key-your-data-centre-cloud-strategy/

Infrastructure as a Service (IaaS)

In this model, the cloud provider holds the infrastructure components that are generally present in an on-premises data centre, including servers, storage and networking hardware. IaaS provides virtualised computing resources over the Internet. Clients can choose not to purchase software or servers, and obtain these resources in an outsourced, on-demand service.

Software as a Service (SaaS)

SaaS allows users to connect as well as use cloud-based apps through the Internet. It provides a complete software solution, which can be purchased from a cloud service provider on a pay-as-you-use basis. The providers rent out the app for use and its users connect to it over the Internet. Office tools like Microsoft Office 365 is an example.

Did You Know?

Around 66% of IT professionals say security is their most significant concern in adopting an enterprise cloud-computing strategy.

Source: 'Cloud Vision 2020: The Future Of The Cloud Study'. https://www.logicmonitor.com/wp-content/uploads/2017/12/LogicMonitor-Cloud-2020-The-Future-of-the-Cloud.pdf

Platform as a Service (PaaS)

Under PaaS, the provider (third party) delivers hardware and software tools to the users through the Internet. A PaaS provider holds the hardware as well as software on its own infrastructure. Therefore, PaaS eliminates the need for users to install in-house hardware and software to develop or run a new application.

Types of Cloud-deployment Models

All clouds are not the same. There are three different ways to deploy cloud-computing resources—public cloud, private cloud and hybrid cloud.

Public cloud

A public cloud is a publicly accessible cloud environment owned by a third-party cloud provider which delivers their computing resources like servers and storage over the Internet. The IT resources on public clouds are usually provisioned through the previously described cloud-delivery models and are generally offered to cloud consumers at a cost or are commercialised via other avenues (such as advertisement). The responsibility of creation and on-going maintenance of the public cloud and its IT resources is of the cloud provider. Ownership and the responsibility for management of all hardware, software and other supporting infrastructure lie with the cloud provider.

Private cloud

In a private cloud, the services and infrastructure are maintained on a private network and the cloud-computing resources are used exclusively by a single business or an organisation. It can be physically located at the company's on-site data centre. An organisation can use cloud-computing technology to centralise access to IT resources by different locations, parts or departments of the company.

Hybrid cloud

Hybrid cloud is a combination of public and private clouds, bound together by technology so that the data and applications can be shared between them. For example, a cloud consumer may choose to move sensitive data to a private cloud and other, less sensitive cloud services to a public cloud. Hybrid cloud gives business entities greater flexibility and more deployment options by allowing data and applications to move between private and public clouds.

Did You Know?

Around 83% of enterprise workload will be in the cloud by 2020, with 41% of enterprise workload run on public cloud platforms, 20% on private clouds and 22% on hybrid cloud platforms.

Source: 'Cloud Vision 2020: The Future Of The Cloud Study'. https://www.logicmonitor.com/wp-content/uploads/2017/12/LogicMonitor-Cloud-2020-The-Future-of-the-Cloud.pdf

How Cloud Computing Works

If you are an executive in a large corporation, your responsibilities would include making sure that all your employees have the right hardware and software that they need to do their jobs. Providing them with computers is not enough, you must purchase the software or acquire the license to give employees the tools they require to do their jobs. Whenever you have a new employee, you must buy more software or make sure your current software license allows another user. This is a lot of work to be concerned about for you at the end of the day.

Cloud computing comes to your rescue. Instead of installing multiple software packages for one computer, you will have to load just one application. That application will enable workers to log into a web-based service which hosts all the programs a user would need for his/her job.

The email account that you use works on the concept of cloud computing.

As a reader of this book, it is safe to assume that you must have an email account with a web-based email service like Hotmail, Yahoo! Mail or Gmail; if so, then you have had some experience with cloud computing. Instead of running an email program on the computer, you log into a web email account remotely. The software or the storage for your email account does not exist on your computer, it is on the service computer's cloud.

Benefits of Using Cloud-computing Services

Cloud computing is a huge shift from the conventional way business organisations think about IT resources. The following are a few common reasons why businesses are adopting cloud-computing services:

Cost

Cloud computing reduces the cost involved in managing and maintaining IT systems. It reduces the cost in the following manner:

- It eliminates the expenditure of buying hardware and software.
- It does away with setting up and running on-site data centres, which have racks of servers and round-the-clock electricity for power and cooling.

- It does not require IT experts for managing the infrastructure.

Therefore, it is more profitable for a company to avail the services offered by cloud-computing software rather than purchasing expensive systems and equipment.

Speed

Cloud-computing services enable users to access huge amounts of computing resources within minutes, and with just a few clicks. This gives business entities a lot of flexibility and lessens their burden of capacity planning.

Global scale

One of the advantages of cloud-computing services is that it delivers the right amount of IT resources—for example, it considers computing power, storage, bandwidth—right when it is required and from the right geographic location. Further, the ability of cloud services to scale up or down depending on a business entity's requirement makes it even more advantageous.

Productivity

Normally on-site data centres require a lot of setting-up time in which they set-up the hardware, patch the software and apart from this, there are other time-consuming IT management chores. However, cloud computing does away with the need for many of these tasks, as a result of which IT teams can spend time on achieving other important business goals.

Performance

Cloud services work through a worldwide network of secure data centres which are periodically updated to the latest generation. Greater economies of scale and reduced network latency are achieved through it.

Did You Know?

Experts predict that 40 zettabytes of data will be held in the cloud by 2020.

Source: 'By 2020, There Will Be 5,200 GB Of Data For Every Person On Earth'. https://www.cio.com/article/2389819/by-2020--there-will-be-5-200-gb-of-data-for-every-person-on-earth.html

Reliability

It makes data backup, recovery from disaster and continuity in business easier and cost-efficient.

Threats of Using Cloud-computing Services

Cloud computing is not all that safe and sound. It comes with certain risks that must be tackled with advanced technology to ensure that cloud computing is a 'safe door option'. Here are a few threats that cloud computing poses:

Security breach

One of the major threats of using cloud computing is security breach or the leak of vital information into the public domain. The leakage or exposure of sensitive information, such as usernames, passwords, credit card numbers, social security and health records, constitutes a data breach. The organisation, and not the cloud-service provider, is ultimately accountable for keeping their data secure.

> *In the event of a data breach, whether intentional or accidental, a company is bound to pay a price, and that too, a heavy one!*

In the event of a breach, whether intentional or accidental, a company is bound to pay a price, and a heavy one at that. It could end up paying hefty fines or even face criminal charges. Thus, organisations must take proactive steps at their end to protect data instead of solely relying on cloud-service providers. It is fair to assume that cloud providers adopt high security measures to protect data on their cloud; however, such measures may prove to be inadequate because of which an organisation must also adopt data-protection mechanisms.

Possible measures include multi-factor authentication processes* and encryption systems at the user end, good password hygiene or access control. Most data breaches and cyber-security attacks are initiated by exploiting vulnerabilities in weak cyber-security systems

---

* Multi-factor authentication (MFA) process is a security system where a user is granted access only after he/she has successfully presented two or more pieces of evidence (or factors) to an authentication mechanism, so as to verify the user's identity for a login/transaction. Usually, the 'factors' for authentication include something only the user knows, something that only the user has/possesses and something only the user is. Example: when we withdraw money from the ATM, it uses a two-factor authentication process (which is a subset of MFA). We are able to withdraw money only after providing our card details (something only the user has) and the PIN code (something only the user knows).

such as easily hackable passwords and poor certificate management.

Natural disasters and bugs

The servers of cloud-computing companies are susceptible to natural disasters such as fires or floods, power outages, or various other unforeseeable circumstances. On one hand, cloud computing makes work more flexible but on the other, any bug or blackout in say, New York, could affect work in Bangalore. A firm in Texas could lose its data if something causes its California-based cloud provider to crash.

Data and applications must be distributed across multiple zones rather than a single zone so as to avoid complete destruction due to situations falling under 'acts of god', that is, unforeseen circumstances beyond human control such as earthquakes, floods, fires, tsunamis, etc. Additionally, organisations must adopt best damage-control practices, business continuity and disaster recovery plans, and enforce appropriate data-backup procedures.

Mistakes

Technology provides innumerable opportunities for employees and managers to learn and develop. But with many individuals, accessing and handling information through a single portal, unintended mistakes can transfer across an entire system which can have a chain effect and cause significant loss. Hence, it is important to have checkpoints to ensure that mistakes and errors can be spotted before they cause damage.

Organisations can avoid data breaches by training their employees on cloud skills and data management in the cloud. Implementation of correct training and management is the best possible way to prevent mistakes occurring in cloud-computing services.

Importance of Cloud Computing in India

With the emergence of e-governance, governments around the world are trying to introduce technology into how they function and strive to deliver services to citizens in a transparent manner. The Indian government's dream of a 'Digital India' envisions the earlier-mentioned aspirations. It aims to create a high-speed digital highway that will impact commerce and create a digital footprint for every individual.

Did You Know?

According to a new study by IDC (International Data Corporation) in India, Salesforce, a cloud-computing company, will create over 1.1 million direct and indirect jobs, contributing $17.2 billion in new business revenues in the Indian GDP by 2022.

Source: 'Cloud Computing To Help Generate 1.1mn Jobs In India By 2022'. https://www.thehindubusinessline.com/info-tech/cloud-computing-to-help-generate-11-mn-jobs-in-india-by-2022-study/article9925120.ece

Governments in well-urbanised places should avail information technology to conduct various functions, such as procurement, loan sanctions, metering, etc. Moving their current IT to the cloud would greatly benefit their attempt to meet the demands of urbanisation. By adopting the cloud model, governments can free up a lot of time and human resources to focus on increasing their roster of services or devising even better delivery mechanisms.

Usage of cloud-computing services in government initiatives like the Aadhar project and the employment generation schemes under the National Rural Employment Guarantee Act (NREGA) can result in material reduction in cost for the government.

Therefore, cloud computing can be the foundation on which governments can create a more trusting environment for e-governance while reaping the benefits of huge cost savings and efficient, easy delivery mechanisms.

Cyber Security in the Cloud

Cloud computing has now become an inevitable part of many companies. Along with its benefits, the cloud has security risks as well. In a world where data breaches occur on an hourly basis, it almost seems that there is no other way for businesses than to wait for an inevitable data breach and thereafter remedy it. Therefore, companies invest a huge amount of money in cyber-security protection mechanisms to ensure their data is safe.

The most common threats and vulnerabilities in cloud-based environments are as follows:

Traffic eavesdropping

This occurs when data is transferred from the cloud consumer to the cloud provider. A malicious service agent passively interrupts the data for illegitimate information-gathering purposes. The aim of this attack is to directly compromise the confidentiality of the data, which can remain undetected for extended periods of time.

Figure 7.1 Traffic Eavesdropper

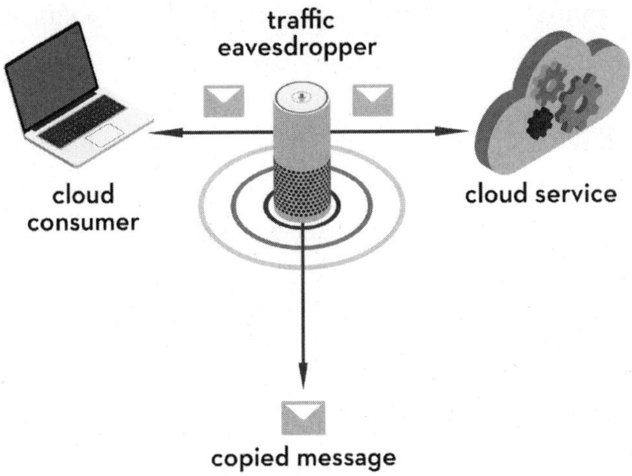

Malicious intermediary

This vulnerability arises when a malicious service agent obstructs and alters the messages. This further leads to potentially compromising a message's confidentiality and integrity. It may also insert harmful data into the message before it gets forwarded to its destination.

Figure 7.2 Malicious Intermediary

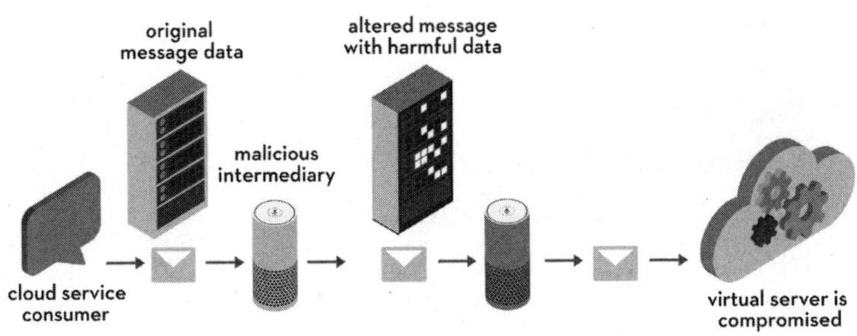

Denial of Service

The denial of service (DoS) attack overloads IT resources to the point where they cannot properly be operated by legitimate users.

Insufficient authorisation

Insufficient authorisation happens when an attacker erroneously gets access to the server. As a result, the attacker gets access to IT resources that are normally protected.

Mechanisms to Protect the Cloud

There are several mechanisms to protect the cloud from security breaches. Some of the mechanisms that are adopted by organisations to protect their vital information in the cloud are:

Encryption

Data by default is coded into a readable format named 'plain text' which is vulnerable to a potentially unauthorised harmful access. The encryption mechanism is a digital coding system, which is used to preserve the confidentiality and integrity of data. It serves the purpose of encoding plaintext data in a protected format which is unreadable.

The 'plain text' is encrypted into a 'cipher text' (encrypted form of the data) using a cipher (a standard algorithm). After encryption is applied to 'plain text', the data is then paired up with several characters known as 'encryption key'. Subsequently, a secret

Step up from ordinary cloud services!
Use cloud services with zero-knowledge encryption!

message is established and shared among authorised users. The use of the encryption key is to decrypt the 'cipher text' back into its original 'plain text' format.

The encryption mechanism can play a vital role in countering activities, such as insufficient authorisation, traffic eavesdropping and other security threats. For example, malicious service agents who try traffic eavesdropping would not be able to decrypt messages in transit if they do not possess the encryption key and would thus not be able to retrieve data from the encrypted message.

> *The encryption mechanism can play a vital role in countering cyber-security threats.*

Encryption is a great way to protect your data, but if you want to add another extra layer of security, you must consider using zero-knowledge cloud storage services. In this system, all your files are locally encrypted in your computer and then uploaded to your cloud provider's servers. This means even the cloud-service provider has no access to your encryption key! Even if anyone attempted to access your files in a zero-knowledge cloud, there would be no way to decrypt it.

Hashing

The hashing mechanism is the most effective form of data protection when a one-way, non-reversible form of data protection is needed. Once a message has been hashed, it is locked, no key is provided for the message to be unlocked. A common practical application of hashing is the storage of passwords.

Hashing technology involves deriving a hashing code or message digest from a message. This hashing code is often of a fixed length and smaller than the original message. Then, the message sender can use the hashing mechanism to attach the message digest to the message. The recipient must apply the same hash function to the message to verify that the produced message digest is the same as the one that accompanied the message.

If the original data is altered, an entirely different message digest is created, clearly indicating that the data has been tampered with. Hashing can be used not only to protect stored cloud data but also to mitigate other forms of cloud threats such as malicious intermediary and insufficient authorisation.

Digital signature

The digital-signature mechanism is a way of proving that data is authentic through authentication and non-repudiation. The process involves assigning a digital signature to a message before its transmission. If any subsequent unauthorised modification takes place, the message is rendered invalid. A digital signature helps in furnishing proof of the fact that the message received is the same as the one created by its true and original sender. This mechanism helps mitigate various security threats.

> *Cloud computing is a revolutionary change in the technical space for storing and accessing data.*

Identity and Access Management (IAM)

The Identity and Access management (IAM) mechanism tracks and controls user identities and access privileges in IT systems. IAM mechanism has four essential components:

authentication, authorisation, user management and credentials management.

Single Sign-on (SSO)

The SSO mechanism allows a cloud-service consumer to be authenticated by a security broker and establish a security context, which persists even while the cloud consumer accesses other cloud services. This eliminates the need for the cloud-service consumer to re-authenticate him/herself after every subsequent request. The SSO's security-broker feature is especially useful when a cloud service consumer needs to access cloud services located on various clouds.

These methods are some ways in which data in the cloud can be protected from any malicious attack or security breach. Technology is changing at a pace that it's hard to keep up, hence it has become important for organisations to always be updated and alert. Cloud computing is a revolutionary change in the technical space for storing and accessing data. Organisations in today's world heavily rely on this system for their effective functioning and therefore, there is a need to ensure that its security is taken care of.

Let us now look into a case that highlights the security vulnerabilities of a cloud storage system.

Case Study—Apple Inc.

The Amazon/Apple social engineering attack in August 2012, which exploited a blind spot between identity verification systems used by Apple and Amazon to remotely delete all information stored on the iPad, iPod and MacBook of technical writer, Mat Honan, can be described in the following sequence of events:

- Hacker discovered Honan's @me.com address on the Internet and found an associated AppleID account.
- Hacker made a call to the customer care service of Amazon in order to add a credit card number to Honan's Amazon account.
- To verify the identity of the customer (supposedly Honan), the Amazon customer care representative asked the hacker to provide the name, billing address and the associated email account. The hacker retrieved this information off the Internet and was thus able to successfully answer the Amazon representative. Thereafter, the Amazon representative added the new credit card onto Honan's account.
- After ending the call, the hacker called the Amazon customer service once again but with a different problem. Hacker said he had lost access to his Amazon account.
- Once again, to verify his identity, the Amazon representative asked for a billing address and a credit card associated with the account. Hacker provided the same billing address and the information of the new credit card, which he added to the account via the previous phone call.
- Since the hacker provided all the correct answers, the Amazon representative added the new email address to Honan's account.
- Hacker logged on to Amazon and requested to reset the password of the email address he just created.
- The hacker had now access to Honan's Amazon account and his credit card information.
- The hacker then called the Apple technical support to reset the password of Honan's @me.com account.
- To verify his identity, the Apple representative asked him account security questions, which the hacker failed to answer. However, the Apple representative provided him with an alternative option.

- The Apple representative only required a billing address and the last four digits of his credit card. Since the hacker had all of this information, he was able to answer and was granted a temporary password.
- The hacker had now access to Honan's Apple iCloud account and remotely deleted all the information from Honan's iPad, iPod and MacBook.

Following this incident, Apple temporarily suspended its support services of permitting a customer to reset an AppleID password over the phone and introduced the iForgot system while promising to working on a much stronger authentication process of identity verification of customers. Amazon suspended its services of changing crucial account information such as email addresses or credit card information via phones.

After having explored important conceptual aspects of cyber security and its interaction with IoT, AI and the cloud in the preceding chapters, it is now time to understand the state of cyber security in India. The following chapter discusses cyber-security management in the Indian context.

8

CYBER-SECURITY MANAGEMENT IN INDIA

Cyber resilience is not solely a concern for companies, it's a societal and government stake.

—Stéphane Nappo, Global Chief Information Security Officer, Société Générale International Banking

The Present Scenario of Cyber-security Management in India

Development in technology has never been obstructed in India. India has a diversified culture of technology in the fields of public and private sectors, banking sector, education sector, research and development, medical field and what not. Each of these sectors, either directly or indirectly, use technology for optimum results. The Information Technology sector is an ever-evolving field. But, the primary concern in the present day is the growing number of cyberattacks in the country.

> *Instances like the WannaCry ransomware, Petya ransomware, several data breaches and the present Aadhar crisis explains the inadequacy of cyber-security measures in India.*

To provide solutions to the government on the issues of cyber security in India, the National Informatics Centre (NIC) was set up as early as 1975. Later, three networks were set up to serve the academic and research communities namely INDONET, ICNET and ERNET.

However, the efforts put up to secure cyberspace in India are not up to the mark. This is evident from the number of cyber-security breaches that have occurred all over India during the past years. Instances like the WannaCry ransomware, Petya ransomware, several data breaches and the present Aadhar crisis explains the inadequacy of cyber-security measures in India as discussed in the upcoming pages. According to the reports of the Indian Computer Emergency Response Team (CERT-In), the total number of cyber incidents that occurred in the years 2014, 2015, 2016 and 2017 are 44,679, 49,455, 50,362 and 53,081 respectively.

Did You Know?

According to the reports of the National Crime Records Bureau (NCRB), a total of 9,622, 11,592 and 12,317 cybercrime cases were registered in India during the years 2014, 2015 and 2016 respectively.

Source: 'Over 53,000 Cyber-security Incidents Observed in 2017'. https://www.thehindubusinessline.com/info-tech/over-53000-cyber-security-incidents-observed-in-2017/article22705876.ece

Business entities are reaping value from data but are neglecting the potential risks associated while doing so. Most companies do not possess an information security management system and the processes; the technological controls for the same are also not in place. Employees working at companies are uninformed about information security. Most of them think it is not required which is evident from the fact that about 45 per cent of attacks are due to the carelessness of employees. Beyond the business sphere, the layman is oblivious to various cyber scams and ignorant of the risks involved while sharing data via online platforms. This is just the tip of the iceberg. Many cybercrime incidents go unreported as either the company is scared to disclose such information due to the fear of ruining their professional reputation or are unaware that a cyber-security breach has occurred.

Why Should Indian Business Entities Pay Heed to Cyber Security?

The digitisation of professional services, the development of Artificial Intelligence (AI) and the development of the Internet of Things (IoT) has propelled technological innovation forward and resulted in information technology becoming an indispensable component of global economic strategy and governance.

Many cybercrime incidents go unreported as either the company is scared to disclose such information due to the fear of ruining their professional reputation or are unaware that a cyber-security breach has occurred.

Ignorant about cyber security? You're in for big trouble!

Business entities do not have any control over the capabilities and acts of cyberattackers but they can take steps to make it difficult for the attackers to access information and their networks. Attackers may be cybercriminals, hacktivists and sometimes even industry competitors and foreign intelligence services who either attempt to gain economic advantage, uncover strategies or damage reputations. A company must consider the potential risks of cyber security very seriously and accordingly make plans to secure its cyberspace.

Few measures which a company can take to maintain cyber security include:

- Providing information to its employees relating to cyber security
- Making use of biometrics
- Establishing strict password requirements
- Avoiding free Wi-Fi
- Installing anti-virus protection for their IT systems

Business leaders are in for a big surprise if they are under an impression that merely backing up their system will safeguard them from any loss or damage of data. Cyberattackers tend to steal personal identity information, rob bank accounts, file fraudulent tax returns and pocket the refunds, commit insurance and healthcare fraud among various other criminal activities.

Did You Know?

According to cyber-security software firm, Symantec, India ranked third in the list of countries where the highest number of cyber threats were detected, and second in terms of targeted attacks in 2017.

Source: 'India Ranks 3rd Among Nations Facing Most Cyber Threats: Symantec'. https://economictimes.indiatimes.com/tech/internet/india-ranks-3rd-among-nations-facing-most-cyber-threats-symantec/articleshow/63616106.cms

Investment in the field of cyber security might be peanuts for big business entities but small business leaders, due to lack of investment or budgetary reasons, tend to ignore cyber-security measures. However, investing in cyber-insurance policies is the smartest move an organisation can make. Cyber and privacy policies cover a huge range of damages caused by a cyberattack. These include fines and penalties, losses resulting from identity theft, notification costs, credit monitoring, etc. When a business entity thinks about the extent of potential liabilities, cyber insurance is worth being a line item in their budget.

Investing in cyber-insurance policies is the smartest move an organisation can make.

Did You Know?

In a 2017 survey, India ranked fourth, globally, as a source of overall malicious activity, and fifth, globally, in terms of detection of ransomware.

Source: 'Internet Security Threat Report'. https://www.symantec.com/content/dam/symantec/docs/reports/istr-22-2017-en.pdf

The use of mobile phones to access data

Another issue that comes before a company is the use of mobile devices to access data. Even if a company has great security policies in the office, many businesses are not successful in providing the same level of security to employees who use phones and tablets. Such devices not only contain valuable data but are also used to access data held in company-owned systems. When it comes to mobile phones, there are significant security loopholes. Phones can be stolen or lost. Employees are also susceptible to opening malicious emails which allows malware to enter their operating system and damage the company's data.

> *The increasing utilisation and incorporation of IT systems and networks in business and corporate entities in India brings both opportunities and dangers.*

Business entities can face issues when they place blind faith in their cloud provider's ability to secure company data, customer information, employees' personal information and any other form of confidential data. While considering a potential cloud vendor, the company should be very confident that the vendor is better equipped to secure the data than the company itself. It is important to know about the cyber-security measures of the cloud vendor. There are numerous cloud providers who agree to provide security at a cheaper rate, but it should be borne in mind that when it comes to securing your company's cyberspace, you truly do get what you pay for!

The increasing utilisation and incorporation of IT systems and networks in business and corporate entities in India bring both opportunities and dangers. With an increase in the number of companies which incorporate cloud-based systems into their infrastructure to move processes online, there is also a substantial increase in cyber-security breaches and the damages such breaches can cause. In the present day, all companies are dependent on information technology to some extent. This makes adopting cyber-security policies a necessity rather than a choice.

Recent Cyber-security Attacks in India

Despite rapid improvement in India's digital infrastructure, user base and accessibility, proper cyber-security measures are yet to keep up with India's digital push, thus exposing several companies to cyberattacks.

According to the Ministry of Electronics and Information Technology, the Indian cyberspace witnessed over 27,000 cyber-security threats in the first half of 2017 alone. These threats range from ransomware attacks, website intrusions or defacement to phishing attacks and data breaches. Some of the major cyber-security attacks are discussed in the following box.

Indian banks breaches

One of the biggest financial data breaches in India, this cyberattack that occurred in 2016, affected popular Indian banks like SBI, HDFC, ICICI, YES Bank and AXIS Bank. To cope up with this cyber crisis, the banks in India had proposed to either replace or change the security codes of about 3.2 million debit cards of the customers who were victimised by the data breach.

It is believed that the breach had its origin in the malware introduced into the systems of Hitachi Payment Service, which provides ATM, point of sale (PoS) and other services. This enabled the cybercriminals to get access to the information and hence steal funds.

Yahoo breach

In December 2016, Yahoo disclosed that a hack, which supposedly occurred in August 2013, affected data associated with more than 1 billion accounts, making this breach one of the company's largest breaches. The data stolen included names, email addresses and other sensitive personal information of customers, thus causing irreparable harm to such customers.

BSNL breach

Bharat Sanchar Nigam Limited, the state-owned telecommunications broadband network in the state of Karnataka, was under a malware attack in 2017. According to reports, the malicious software affected hundreds of modems with default 'admin-admin' username and password combination. As a result, the modems infected with the malware could not be used to connect to the Internet. Following this breach, BSNL issued an advisory notice to all its broadband customers requesting them to change their default router username as well as passwords.

Reliance Jio crisis

Reliance Jio, the trending network service provider was also a victim of a data breach in the year 2017. A website with the name magicapk.com provided access to the personal details of Jio customers by just typing the user's Jio number. Reports stated that the website displayed the name, email address and the Aadhar number of the customers. The website was later taken down after it went viral.

Locky ransomware

After India was hit by the Locky ransomware, CERT-In issued an advisory notice urging users not to open any emails with attachments from anonymous senders. The advisory notice revealed that the ransomware spreads through a massive spam campaign. According to reports, over 23 million messages were sent in this phishing campaign.

Locky encrypts files on victims' PCs by adding a .locky file extension. The attacker then demands ransom to unlock the files so that the user can access it. Locky asks for a bitcoin payment in order to recover the files. According to a recent study by Google, Chainalysis, UC (University of California) San Diego and the NYU (New York University) Tamdom School of Engineering, the Locky ransomware extorted more than $7.8 million in payments.

As a response to the ransomware, CERT-In advised both citizens and corporate entities to not open emails with subjects like 'please print', 'documents', 'photo', 'images', 'scans' and 'pictures'.

Petya ransomware

When the attack occurred, the researchers stated that it was not necessarily ransomware but rather a wiper, that is, the aim of the malware was to delete all data. The idea of this attack was to cause massive destruction of data and not just to make financial gains.

WannaCry ransomware

About 2 lakh computers across the world were affected by the WannaCry virus. India was the third worst-hit nation by the ransomware as reportedly more than 40,000 computers were affected by it. Computers running on older versions of Microsoft operating systems like XP are most vulnerable to cyberattacks like WannaCry. The virus used to lock the users' devices and prevent them from accessing data and software until a certain ransom was paid to the attacker. Cybercriminals demanded a ransom of $300 in crypto-currencies like bitcoin for unlocking the device and enabling the user to access the data.

India was affected by this attack since most of the private as well as public organisations in India still use outdated operating systems which are easily hackable. Several Indian companies ended up paying the ransom demanded by WannaCry.

Former IB chief, after WannaCry occurred, attributed India's vulnerability to a cyber catastrophe like WannaCry to the following reasons:

- Non-updation of software and hardware
- Lack of cyber hygiene
- Under-reporting of breaches

Aadhar crisis

It was asserted that *The Tribune*, a daily newspaper in January 2018, purchased a service which was offered by anonymous sellers through WhatsApp that provided unrestricted access to details of more than 1 billion Aadhaar numbers created in India by just paying an amount of ₹500. This security breach signifies poor security practices, putting people at risk of financial frauds as well as identity thefts. There were also numerous flaws in the Aadhar app. However, the former UIDAI (Unique Identification Authority of India) DG denied the allegation of such breaches.

The most recent Aadhar data leak was unearthed by French cyber-security researcher Baptiste Robert, known online as Elliot Alderson, who reported on 19 February 2019 that Aadhaar data of about 6.7 million dealers, distributors and customers had been leaked by Indane, a Liquefied Petroleum Gas brand developed and owned by Indian Oil Corporation. The Indane database leaked names, addresses and Aadhaar numbers of such individuals.

Government's cyber vulnerabilities affect private sector in IRINN hack

A recent report by Seqrite Intelligence Labs, the enterprise security solutions brand of Quick Heal Technologies, disclosed an advertisement which they discovered on the Darknet (see Chapter 2). The advertisement announced secret access to the servers and databases of over 6,000 Indian organisations, including internet service providers (ISPs) as well as public and private sector organisations. The hacker offered this information in exchange for 15 bitcoins (equivalent to approximately $73,000). Further, the hacker also offered to execute further cyberattacks against the listed companies for an undisclosed price.

Seqrite Cyber Intelligence Labs, along with its partner seQtree InfoServices, reported that the Indian Registry for Internet Names and Numbers (IRINN), which comes under the aegis of the National Internet Exchange of India, was compromised.

Following the discovery of the advertisement, Seqrite and seQtree teams began gathering background research on the hacker but were ultimately unable to identify the cybercriminal. The research team then posed as an interested buyer and contacted the hacker for further details. The hacker shared a sample of their stolen data, which included an email address of a prominent Indian technology firm and information linked to the Indian government.

According to Seqrite Intelligence Labs, this hacker may have the capacity to create serious service outages in India. The entities affected by the data breach included the Bombay Stock Exchange, the Reserve Bank of India, the Indian Space Research Organisation, Wipro, Mastercard, Visa, Hathaway, IDBI Bank and Ernst & Young.

According to researchers, the seller claimed to have the ability to tamper the IP allocation pool, which could potentially result in a serious outage or distributed denial of service (DDoS) condition.

Did You Know?

Altaf Halde, managing director, Kaspersky Lab, South Asia, stated that India was third on the total number of attacks by WannaCry globally.

Source: 'India Saw 48,000 WannaCry Ransomware Attacks, 3rd Highest In the World'. https://localpress.co.in/trending/india-saw-48000-wannacry-ransomware-attacks-3rd-highest-world/

Is India Equipped to Tackle Cyber Breaches?

After the WannaCry and Petya attacks, Ravi Shankar Prasad, the then information technology minister of India, claimed that cyberattacks against India were at a minimum. However, statistics prove that the Indian cyberspace continues to be a favourite playground for cybercriminals.

Did You Know?

An independent research by Quick Heal Technologies, a cyber-security firm, revealed that India was the third worst-hit nation by WannaCry, which affected about 48,000 computers, with most incidents in West Bengal.

Source: 'India Third Worst Hit Nation By Ransomware WannaCry; Over 40,000 Computers Affected'. https://economictimes.indiatimes.com/tech/internet/india-third-worst-hit-nation-by-ransomware-wannacry-over-40000-computers-affected/articleshow/58707260.cms

India was ranked the fifth most-vulnerable country for cyber breaches in 2016 by Symantec's Internet Cyber Security Threat Report of 2017. The year 2017 witnessed 29 major data-breach incidents, the most common being identity theft. According to the Breach Level Index study by the digital security firm, Gemalto, data theft increased by 78.3 per cent in India in 2017, with about 3.24 million records stolen, lost or exposed. According to a joint study by IBM Security and Ponemon Institute in 2017, the average cost of a data breach in India rose nearly 8 per cent year-on-year to ₹11.9 crore ($1.7 million). As per government data, over 22,000 Indian websites, including 114 government portals were hacked between April 2017 and January 2018.

For instance, in May 2017, the personal data of millions of Indians registered with the Employees' Provident Fund Organisation was leaked. Further, in 2017, the mean time to identify a data breach increased to 188 days in India from 170 days in 2016, whereas the time taken to contain them increased from 72 to 78 days. Also, 2017 experienced an increasing incidence of cybercrimes known as *nuisance attacks* which were unseen in 2016, and involved compromising of basic information such as names, addresses and/or phone numbers. The industries that experienced the largest number of data-breach incidents were government (28 per cent), retail (21 per cent), education (17 per cent) and healthcare (7 per cent). In terms of the number of records lost, stolen or compromised, the most targeted sectors were government (62 per cent) and technology (37 per cent)

According to the reports of a survey conducted by a British security software and hardware company, Sophos, India was the third worst-hit nation by cyberattacks in 2018 among the 12 countries surveyed, and nearly 76 per cent of Indian businesses suffered. Company servers (39 per cent threats), company networks (34.5 per cent) and mobile devices (18 per cent) were found to be the most vulnerable spots. It was reported that about 14 per cent of the IT managers who faced a cyberattack could not determine the point of breach, while 17 per cent were clueless about the existence of the threat before detection. Further, according to a 2018 study by another British cyber-security company, Comparitech, India was ranked 15th in a cyber-security ranking of 60 nations, where rank 1 meant least secure and rank 60 the most secure, thereby implying that India is among the worst countries in the world with respect to internet safety. These data go on to show that India is a 'cyber-security laggard', and malware-infected mobile phones and desktops were identified as the primary reasons for the same.

We all know that numbers don't lie, and the earlier mentioned facts and figures prove that India needs to improve its digital-security architecture and protocol.

How Can Foreign Businesses Protect Themselves in India?

The reluctance of the Indian government in acknowledging its own vulnerabilities to cyberattacks and the country's increasing plight in the invisible hands of cyberattackers, may soon spell the demise of its aspirations of being 'Digital India'. It is imperative that foreign companies carrying on businesses in India take adequate data protection and cyber-security measures.

Foreign companies entering the Indian market should make cyber security top priority and invest in strong and reliable cyber-security policies and measures to be successful.

Did You Know?

Globally, India was ranked as the seventh most-impacted nation by Petya ransomware, according to Symantec reports.

Source: 'India Among Top 10 Victims of Petya Ransomware Attack'. https://www.thehindubusinessline.com/info-tech/india-among-top-10-victims-of-petya-ransomware-attack/article9741461.ece

When designing a cyber-security policy/plan, businesses must take into consideration the following important points:

- **Risk analysis**: The first and foremost step in developing a cyber-security plan for an organisation is risk analysis. An organisation must identify its vulnerabilities, weak points and usual entry spots for hackers, and take necessary steps to eliminate such risks. Organisations need to acquire an in-depth understanding of their cyber-security risks and accordingly implement strong hardware, office and internet-security policies.
- **Regular software and hardware updates**: In order to keep cyberattackers at bay, it is imperative for an organisation to invest in a reputed software solution which offers frequent anti-virus updates. Further, all employees must be trained to install necessary software updates on a real-time basis. Also, the main servers must always be equipped with the latest versions of firewall and anti-virus systems. These preventive measures are expected to significantly reduce the feasibility of any form of cyberattack.
- **Cloud storage**: A centralised form of data storage is highly susceptible to cyberattacks, and thus, can be easily corrupted and/or destroyed. Hence, organisations should consider storing their data in a decentralised manner, such as cloud storage. Data storage across various cloud platforms substantially reduces its vulnerability. Further, when choosing a cloud-service provider, organisations must opt for cloud providers who ensure advanced cyber-security measures and assure that all crucial information has multiple layers of protection.

- **Data encryption**: Organisations must consider encrypting their data. Moreover, when outsourcing their data storage functions to a remote cloud-service provider, it is desirable that an organisation chooses a cloud provider with encryption services. Encryption of company information on hard drives prevents unauthorised access.
- **IT support**: Organisations must build a robust defence system to protect its business from cyber threats and ensure business continuity and disaster recovery. This may be achieved by building an in-house IT support department or outsourcing its IT services to established service providers.

Initiatives a Company Should Take to Prevent Cyber-security Breaches

Updating

The first and foremost step that any business entity should take to prevent cyber breaches is updating its computer systems. Many people do not consider updating systems to be important for securing their cyberspace, but it should be borne in mind that outdated systems are most vulnerable to cyberattacks. The WannaCry ransomware attacked most of the systems working on Windows XP version.

Apart from updating the computer systems, the anti-virus used to protect the system also needs to be updated in a timely manner. Outdated anti-virus is futile and hence cannot prevent a cyber crisis.

Backup

Having a data backup is the safest way of avoiding the aftermath of a cyberattack. Most of the attacks either erase the data or ask for a ransom to resume access to data. In such situations, companies can avoid becoming prey to attacks by backing up their data offline, that is, in a hard disk or a pen-drive.

Shredding files

The business organisation should always remember to shred all the files and folders before disposing of storage equipment. Merely deleting files or reformatting hard drives does not erase data. Certain applications can retrieve information after formatting. There are certain software types which are designed for permanently wiping the hard drive and CDs, DVDs and other portable media. Also, one should be mindful of photocopy machines, as many of these scan a document before copying. So, to clear data from the machine, appropriate settings should be changed.

Unencrypted files

The business institution should ban devices, which are unencrypted like laptops and other portable devices as they are most prone to attack. Encryption of all data transmissions should be made mandatory. This includes data 'at rest' and 'in motion'. Also, a company should avoid using unreliable Wi-Fi networks as they may permit interception of data.

Password

Many security experts lay emphasis on regularly changing the password for better cyber security. Also, the password should be strong and difficult to predict. In the past, companies rarely interfered with how often the employees changed their passwords, but the recent trend of cyber breaches has changed their perception about such interference. Most of the companies now advise their employees to timely change the passwords used in the systems.

A good password should be really difficult to crack. The use of upper-case letters, numbers, special characteristics, etc., while formulating a password helps in making it unpredictable.

Also, there are few automating systems which reduce the risk of leaking of sensitive information by regularly checking the password settings, server and firewall configuration. Business institutions can also implement password protection and 'time-out' functions (requires re-login after periods of inactivity) for all computers. All the employees should be trained to never leave laptops unattended.

Security team

Every business entity should have a cyber-security team in place, which should be able to identify suspicious network activity and should be prepared in case there is an attack on the network. Security teams can control the network by periodically checking security controls.

The security team should also track the movement of data within the organisational network to prevent any unintentional use of sensitive information. A cyber-security specialist should be appointed and the employees should be educated about past events of data breaches.

Security training

Many cyber-security surveys revealed that employees are the weakest link in the data-security chain. Thus, the best way to prevent a cyber breach is to educate employees about the current trends of data breaches, provide them privacy and security training and teach them the measures they should adopt to prevent a breach.

Every business firm should put its best foot forward in training its employees on how to encrypt data, how to formulate strong, unpredictable passwords, how to file and store data as well as how to avoid malware. Further, employees should only be allowed to access the websites within the scope of their daily duties and not others.

However, despite training, employees often open suspicious emails every now and then that have the potential to download viruses. It is a general conception that one training class is enough to learn all about cyber security but this is not the case. Regular classes on cyber security should be conducted. In those sessions, employees should be educated about what types of information are sensitive or confidential and what their responsibilities are to protect that data. The company should also formulate a written policy on privacy and data security and communicate the same to all its employees.

Breach-response plan

Even after having a highly functional security team and well-educated employees, the hackers can still find a way to enter into the system and steal confidential data. So, having a breach- response plan will help in triggering quick

> *Developing a comprehensive cyber-breach preparedness plan is beneficial for both the employees and the employer in understanding the potential damages that could occur.*

response to data breaches and help in the reduction of any damage arising therefrom.

The breach-response plan should contain steps involving notifying the concerned staff or the agency who could contain the breach. Developing a comprehensive breach-preparedness plan is beneficial for both the employees and the employer in understanding the potential damages that could occur. The employer should be very transparent about the breach; the employees deserve to know the truth. The response plan should begin with an evaluation of exactly what was lost and when, and finding out who was responsible whenever possible. By taking swift, decisive actions, a company can limit damages and restore public and employee trust.

Limited access to valuable data

In earlier times, every employee had access to all the files on their computers but nowadays companies are learning to limit access to more critical data. After all, there's no reason why a mailroom employee should have access to a customer's financial information. When a company limits who can view certain documents, it can narrow down the pool of employees who might accidentally click on a harmful link.

Conduct regular tests and audits

One of the most effective ways to protect oneself from a data breach is to find out if you are vulnerable to one. This can be achieved by conducting regular tests and audits. By doing so, a company can get proof whether the data is secure or not and thus minimise the risk of a breach.

Other measures

- No employee should click on any unknown attachment even if the email is from a known sender.
- Extra precaution should be taken while using the systems at the workplace as certain viruses can rapidly spread through intranet (LAN).
- While browsing, one should steer clear from unsafe websites and employ essential filters on the browser.
- A business organisation should ban shifting data from one device to another external device as losing removable media will put the data on the disk under risk.
- Every employee should keep business and personal accounts separate by having separate emails for business, personal and banking.
- A company should refrain from using social-security numbers as employee ID or client account numbers; it should instead develop another ID system for the same.
- Every company enters into business agreements with a wide array of third-party vendors. It is crucial now than ever to know who these people are. A company should choose the third party very carefully as then it puts crucial data of the entity into risk.

Surviving a Data-security Breach: Response

After a business entity discovers that it has been a victim to a data breach, the first question that comes to the mind is what now? What is to be done? After the company gets to know about the cyber crisis, the very first thing it needs to do is breathe and not to panic. Maybe the breach is not so severe and the information retrieved by the cybercriminals is not sensitive information of the company. Nonetheless, the organisation should respond in the following manner:

Evaluate the loss

Questions like—what exactly has been lost, what did the cybercriminal manage to steal from the company, is that information significant for the company's future—need to be answered. In the process of evaluating losses, if the company does not have a serious IT department, it should hire a professional team for the same.

Isolate the network for sometime

As soon as the management comes to know about the crisis, it should change the credentials for important online accounts and servers. The servers, machines and parts of systems which contain important information should be isolated as soon as possible.

Suspect the human element

The employees are the weakest link in the system. It is difficult to deal with people because of their lack of knowledge or awareness. It may happen that even after multiple reminders about updating systems, changing passwords, not opening unidentified emails, they might commit a mistake, either intentional or out of negligence, which could cost a huge loss to the company. Therefore, it is essential to find out through whose system the breach crept in and spread throughout the entire company network.

Learn from the breach

After a breach occurs and the company investigates into the matter, it should try to learn from the crisis: What were the loopholes in the system which caused the breach? Were the employees not trained enough to follow basic guidelines for a safer cyberspace?

Train the employees

Training the employees on various aspects of cyber-security breaches should be the next step a company should take. They should be told about the changing trends of cyberattacks, what to do and what not to do for ensuring safer cyberspace, etc. Since human errors and negligence also significantly lead to cyber crisis, this step becomes very crucial.

> *An efficient IT department can:*
>
> - *Avoid cyber breaches*
> - *Detect cyber breaches*
> - *Help in mitigating losses*

The IT department

An efficient IT department can avoid cyber breaches, detect cyber breaches and help in mitigating the losses. Thus, it is recommended by cyber-security experts that the IT department of the organisation should be highly trained and functional and that the organisation should invest in the field of cyber security.

Steps Involved in Drafting an Effective Cyber-security Policy

Secure senior management buy-in

If there are few IT professionals in the business entity, they could help in training fellow employees about best security practices for avoiding a cyberattack. But, in order to have the resources to design the policy and the authority to enforce it, there is a need for management too.

Determining security guidelines

The reason for having a cyber-security policy is that there are a lot of things to track, irrespective of whether an entity is big or small, and the landscape is constantly evolving as both the technology as well as cybercriminals are becoming more advanced. Only the senior managers of a company are aware of the individualistic needs of the organisation, but there are certain general needs and to safeguard those, the following areas must be investigated:

- Which industry regulations should be complied with?
- What data needs protection and how should it be stored and transferred?
- Which business software needs to be maintained and updated to ensure security?
- Who will be managing the cyber-security policy?
- What is the penalty for wilful non-compliance of guidelines?

Once these questions are answered, it doesn't take much time to draft the cyber-security policy.

Train your employees on cyber-security policies such as:

- *Strong password training*
- *Responsible email usage*
- *Data-incident reporting*
- *Spam and phishing training*
- *Device management*

Educating the employees

The next step in the process of cyber-securing the organisation is communicating a new cyber-security policy to the employees. It should be ensured that they understand the relevant details such as their roles and responsibilities, the manner of implementation and the consequences of not adhering to the cyber-security policy. Organisations must train their employees on best cyber-security practices, such as strong password training, phishing and spam training, reporting of cyber intrusions, device management, remote access and Wi-Fi training as well as acceptable-use policy. Training employees to recognise cyber threats can go a long way to prevent cyberattacks. Regular refresher courses must be conducted and employees must be taught responsible management of company data, document management, responsible email usage and overall cyber-protection policies.

Monitor and update your policy

After the cyber-security policy is up and functional, there is another step that should be taken—it should be updated regularly to include any changes in the business, technology and regulations. The best way to do so is by setting a timeline for when the policy needs to be re-evaluated.

Quick Tips on What to Include in the Cyber-security Policies

Drafting a cyber-security policy for a company means coverage of a multitude of issues. Such a policy needs to be customised according to the company's individual needs and requirements. One needs to keep legal, business and privacy/security objectives in mind while drafting is in process. The policy so drafted should be developed, reviewed and maintained regularly. The business entity should ensure that the policy guides the employees in the fields of:

- Technology
- Information

- Online transactions
- Online interactions

An organisation needs to keep legal, business and data privacy objectives in mind while drafting a cyber-security policy.

This way employees can understand the significant role they play in the organisation's security.

Generally, a cyber-security policy should include guidelines in the following broad areas:

Password

- Manner of storing passwords correctly
- Requisite frequency of updating passwords
- The necessity of having unique passwords for different logins

Email standards

- Circumstances when work email address may be shared
- The necessity of opening email attachments from trusted contacts and businesses only
- The process to block junk, spam and scam emails
- The necessity of deleting and reporting suspicious-looking emails

Handling of sensitive data

- Circumstances when sensitive data may be shared with others
- The necessity of storing physical files in a locked room or drawer
- The proper identification of sensitive data

- The need to destroy any sensitive data when it is no longer required

Locking computers and devices

- The need to physically shut down computers and mobile devices when they aren't in use
- The necessity of locking screens when they are left unattended

A cyber-security policy should include guidelines on:

- *Password*
- *Email standards*
- *Handling of sensitive data*
- *Locking computers and devices*
- *Handling of removable devices*
- *Handling of technology*
- *Social media access standards*
- *Handling incidents*

Handling of removable devices

- The method to protect data stored on removable devices like USB sticks
- The necessity of restricting the use of removable devices to prevent malware from being installed
- The importance of scanning removable devices before connecting them to the systems

Handling of technology

- The manner of remote access
- The manner of device storage when not in use
- The method of reporting a theft or loss of a work device

Social media and internet-access standards

- The kind of business information that can be shared on social media channels

- The channels and newsletters which are appropriate for employees to sign when using their work email account
- Whether social media platforms should be accessed during work hours

Managing incidents

- The manner of responding to a cyber incident
- Necessary actions to be taken
- The roles and responsibilities of various parties in dealing with the cyberattack

Challenges in the Field of Cyber Security in India

Securing Indian cyberspace is easier said than done. There are numerous barriers to the process. These hurdles are either faced by the business entities or are caused by them.

Did You Know?

As per the reports of CERT-In, Indian organisations reported more than 53,000 security incidents in 2017 alone—a security incident reported every 10 minutes.

Source: 'India Sees One Cyber-security Incident Every 10 Minutes'. https://www.paladion.net/india-sees-one-cyber-security-incident-every-10-minutes

Under-reporting of cases

It is a well-known fact that when a cyber breach occurs, most of the business institutions do not disclose the occurrence of such a breach. The reason behind such a decision is simple—they do not want to lose their reputation in the market. When a cyber crisis occurs, the reputation of the company is at stake, as its customers will have an impression that they have rendered their personal information in wrong hands. This is the main reason behind under-reporting of cyber-security breaches.

It is mandatory for banks (according to the RBI mandate) and a few listed companies to disclose cyberattacks, but very few comply with it. When the world was attacked by WannaCry ransomware, India was one among the worst-hit countries, but very few companies reported being affected by WannaCry. This situation leads to calculating false estimates relating to cyber breaches. Thus, under-reporting of cyber breaches is the biggest challenge that India faces.

Investment in research and development

India does not take investment in research and development in various fields seriously. Cyber security is one among those fields. Cyberspace is something which keeps evolving from time to time. There are new technological advancements, new forms of breaches, new means to prevent such breaches, etc. India is lagging in knowledge of these areas. The government, as well as individual companies, should invest more in research of these areas.

However, India being a developing nation cannot be expected to invest a huge sum of money in research and development. Also, it is illogical to expect small companies to invest into research. Thus, huge established business entities should take the duty upon themselves.

Lack of awareness

The plight is such that many small business entities do not have any idea that they are under a cyber threat. They just choose to overlook the most evident facts.

Despite cybercrime rates increasing day by day, the government as well as private-sector organisations do not take adequate measures to be aware of the recent trends in cyberspace. Boards of organisations continue to display obliviousness and treat cyber security as an IT problem, rather than a human problem, where in fact, the 'human factor' is the largest contributor to cyber breaches.

Did You Know?

A study conducted by Fortinet, a cyber-security company, revealed that about 94% of IT experts in India believe that information-security practices in Indian organisations are insufficient and do not safeguard from cybercrimes.

Source: '94% Of Cyber-attacks Are Caused By Lack Of Infosecurity Awareness Training. Is Your Organisation Safe?' https://yourstory.com/2017/11/94pc-cyber-attacks-caused-lack-infosecurity-awareness

Lack of trained and qualified manpower

India lags both in terms of quality as well as quantity in cyber- security-related skilled workers. There is a manpower deficit when it comes to tackling a cyber incident. It is recommended by cyber-security experts that every firm should have a cyber-security team and a cyber-security expert to help educate the employees about cyber threats as well as track the company's data for any unusual activity (signs of cyberattack). However, India lacks people who are qualified and trained enough for the job. It should be noted that cyberattack is not an IT issue and cannot be handled properly by a normal IT professional; individuals trained specifically in cyber security can be helpful in both preventing and reducing the impact of a cyber breach. Due to this reason, many private-sector organisations either don't have a cyber-security team or appoint a team which is not qualified enough to comprehend the impact.

Lack of coordination between organisations regulating cyber security in India

There are various initiatives taken by the government in the field of cyber security. Also, various organisations were set up to implement the same. The Indian Computer Emergency Response Team (CERT-In), the National Cyber Coordination Centre (NCCC), the National Critical Information Infrastructure Protection Centre (NCIIPC), etc., are a few agencies working in this field. But, these organisations or agencies are not coordinating with each other. Lack of coordination between them has led to a reduction in efficiency of cyber-security initiatives.

How to overcome these challenges?

The list of challenges faced is never ending; hence, it becomes difficult to find a solution to these challenges. There are certain hurdles which can be tackled with the help of a few collaborative efforts from the government as well as business entities.

The issue of lack of investment in the field of cyber security can be tackled by the government's initiatives to invest in securing the Indian cyberspace. With an aim to deal with the increasing incidence of cyberspace threats, the Indian government in 2016 decided to set up a ₹1,000 crore fund, administered by a committee headed by the national security adviser, Ajit Doval. This committee will look into areas of research and development of cyber-security products and systems.

Another issue of lack of trained cyber-security staff can be addressed by building indigenous expertise in security technologies, which would also help local firms to tap a larger pie of the country's digital-security technology budget.

Further, in 2015, The National Association of Software and Services Companies (NASSCOM) and Symantec signed a Memorandum of Understanding (MoU) for 'Building Cyber-security Skills'. This purpose of this initiative was to develop 'world-class skilled and certified professionals'.

The issue of under-reporting of cases can be handled by educating the employees about cyber breaches and how to mitigate the consequences, and by making it mandatory for most of the companies to report cyberattacks, failing which, there should be huge penalty imposition.

In the last few decades, India has carved a niche for itself in information technology. Apart from various public-sector organisations, most of the Indian banking industry and financial institutions have embraced IT to a large extent. With the optimal use of technology in various sectors there comes an increasing threat to Indian cyberspace. To ensure that the Indian cyberspace is secure, the government, as well as the private sector, should jointly make cyber security a priority. India is in dire need of a cyber-security renaissance that promotes cyber hygiene and a security-centric corporate culture.

REFERENCES

1. Rouse, M., and C. Clark. 2018. 'Cybersecurity'. Available at: https://searchsecurity.techtarget.com/definition/cybersecurity
2. *University of Central Arkansas*. 'What Is Malware?' Available at: https://uca.edu/ist/knowledgebase/what-is-malware/
3. Rijnetu, I. 2018. '13+ Warning Signs that Your Computer Is Malware-Infected'. Available at: https://heimdalsecurity.com/blog/warning-signs-operating-system-infected-malware/
4. *Kaspersky*. 'Learn about Malware and How to Protect All Your Devices against It'. Available at: https://www.kaspersky.co.in/resource-center/preemptive-safety/what-is-malware-and-how-to-protect-against-it
5. Lord, N. 2018. 'What Is a Phishing Attack? Defining and Identifying Different Types of Phishing Attacks'. Available at: https://digitalguardian.com/blog/what-phishing-attack-defining-and-identifying-different-types-phishing-attacks
6. *We Live Security*. 2016. '5 Simple Ways You Can Protect Yourself from Phishing Attacks'. Available at: https://www.welivesecurity.com/2016/09/22/5-simple-ways-can-protect-phishing-attacks/
7. *Acunetix*. 'What Is SQL Injection (SQLi) and How to Prevent It'. Available at: https://www.acunetix.com/websitesecurity/sql-injection/
8. *AppliCure Technologies*. 'Prevent Denial of Service (DoS) Attacks'. Available at: http://www.applicure.com/solutions/prevent-denial-of-service-attacks

9. *Wordfence*. 2017. 'How to Prevent Cross Site Scripting Attacks'. Available at: https://www.wordfence.com/learn/how-to-prevent-cross-site-scripting-attacks/
10. *Deloitte*. 2016. 'Cyber Crisis Management: Readiness, Response, and Recovery'. Available at: https://www2.deloitte.com/content/dam/Deloitte/global/Documents/Risk/gx-cm-cyber-pov.pdf
11. Cheriyan, R. 2017. 'Massive Data Breaches and Cyber Threats in India'. Available at: https://www.india-briefing.com/news/massive-data-breaches-cyber-threats-india-15405.html/
12. *ARN*. 'Top 10 Most Notorious Cyber Attacks in History'. Available at: https://www.arnnet.com.au/slideshow/341113/top-10-most-notorious-cyber-attacks-history/
13. Evans, M. 2015. 'Hackers Steal £650 Million in World's Biggest Bank Raid'. Available at: https://www.telegraph.co.uk/news/uknews/crime/11414191/Hackers-steal-650-million-in-worlds-biggest-bank-raid.html
14. Bell, K. 2016. 'Yahoo Confirms over 1 billion User Accounts Have Been Hacked'. Available at: https://www.cultofmac.com/458345/yahoo-confirms-over-1-billion-user-accounts-have-been-hacked/
15. Schwartz, M.J. 2017. '7 Facts: "Vault 7" CIA Hacking Tool Dump by WikiLeaks'. Available at: https://www.bankinfosecurity.com/7-facts-vault-7-cia-hacking-tool-dump-by-wikileaks-a-9766
16. McAuley, J. 2017. 'Campaign Emails from French President Macron Part of Latest Political Leak'. Available at: https://www.washingtonpost.com/world/europe/campaign-emails-from-french-president-macron-part-of-latest-political-leak/2017/07/31/933935e0-75d7-11e7-9eac-d56bd5568db8_story.html?noredirect=on&utm_term=.92b8eb4964b9
17. Shukla, S., and P. Bhakta. 2016. '3.2 Million Debit Cards Compromised; SBI, HDFC Bank, ICICI, YES Bank and Axis Worst Hit'. Available at: https://economictimes.indiatimes.com/industry/banking/finance/banking/3-2-million-debit-

cards-compromised-sbi-hdfc-bank-icici-yes-bank-and-axis-worst-hit/articleshow/54945561.cms

18. Hastreiter, N. 'How AI and Blockchain Will Shape the Future of Cybersecurity'. Available at: https://www.futureofeverything.io/future-of-cybersecurity/
19. Gupta, K. 2018. 'Cybercrimes Cost Firms $600 Billion Last Year: McAfee Report'. Available at: https://www.livemint.com/Technology/fZn1bmxjRGM2Qwxo0ErEUK/Cybercrimes-cost-firms-600-billion-last-year-McAfee-report.html?utm_source=scroll&utm_medium=referral&utm_campaign=scroll
20. Mardisalu, R. 2019. '14 Most Alarming Cyber Security Statistics in 2019'. Available at: https://thebestvpn.com/cyber-security-statistics-2019/
21. Bisson, D. 2016. '6 Common Phishing Attacks and How to Protect against Them'. Available at: https://www.tripwire.com/state-of-security/security-awareness/6-common-phishing-attacks-and-how-to-protect-against-them/
22. Leyden, J. 2018. 'Phishing Fraudsters Set Their Sights on Online Storage Portals'. Available at: https://portswigger.net/daily-swig/phishing-fraudsters-set-their-sights-on-online-storage-portals
23. *Reinsurance News.* 2017. 'Total WannaCry Losses Pegged at $4 Billion'. Available at: https://www.reinsurancene.ws/total-wannacry-losses-pegged-4-billion/
24. Klinder, B. 2017. 'Startups Need to Plan for Cyber Security Implications from Day 1'. Available at: https://hackernoon.com/startups-need-to-plan-for-cyber-security-implications-from-day-1-8ed61c5abac8?gi=365044a4c11
25. Lahanas, S. 2015. '10 Reasons Why You Need a Cybersecurity Plan'. Available at: https://insights.dice.com/2015/02/16/10-reasons-need-cybersecurity-plan/
26. Sukumar, A.M. 2016. 'Upgrading India's Cyber Security Architecture'. Available at: http://www.thehindu.com/opinion/columns/upgrading-indias-cyber-security architecture/article8327987.ece

27. *Sungard Availability Services*. 'The Consequences of a Cyber Security Breach'. Available at: https://www.sungardas.com/en/cyber-security-advice/articles/the-consequences-of-a-cyber-security-breach.html
28. *DeVry University*. 2014. 'The Top 5 Cyber Security Threats That Could Affect Your Life'. Available at: https://www.devry.edu/blog/2014/02/top-5-cyber-security-threats-that-could-affect-your-life.html
29. Kadam, 2015. A. 'Why Cyber Security Is Important for Digital India'. Available at: https://www.firstpost.com/business/why-cyber-security-is-important-for-digital-india-2424380.html
30. *Reserve Bank of India*. 2016. 'Cyber Security Framework in Banks'. Available at: https://rbidocs.rbi.org.in/rdocs/notification/PDFs/NT41893F697BC1D57443BB76AFC7AB56272EB.PDF
31. Varghese, S. 'How Secure is Your Small Business from Cyber Attacks?' Available at: https://www.timedoctor.com/blog/small-business-cyber-attacks/
32. *IAS Score*. 'Global Cyber Security Index 2017'. Available at: http://iasscore.in/ias-prelims/global-cyber-security-index-2017
33. *ASG Information Technologies*. 'Cyber Security Myths: 5 Common Myths and Why They Aren't True'. Available at: http://www.asgct.com/cyber-security-myths-5-common-myths-and-why-they-arent-true/
34. *Sentryo*. 2016. 'Cybersecurity: Unraveling 6 Common Myths'. Available at: https://www.sentryo.net/cybersecurity-unraveling-6-common-myths/
35. Keeney, P. 2017. 'Unraveling Six Myths of Cybersecurity'. Available at: https://www.stambaughness.com/blog/unraveling-six-myths-cybersecurity/
36. Berman, S. 2013. 'Why Planning Is Key to Combating Cyber Threats and Attacks'. Available at: https://www.theguardian.com/media-network/media-network-blog/2013/sep/06/planning-key-cyber-threat-attack
37. Palmer, D. 2018. 'What Is Malware? Everything You Need to Know about Viruses, Trojans and Malicious Software'.

Available at: https://www.zdnet.com/article/what-is-malware-everything-you-need-to-know-about-viruses-trojans-and-malicious-software/

38. Fernandes, T. 2016. '5 Scary Facts You Didn't Know about the Internet!' Available at: https://www.globalo.com/5-scary-facts-you-didnt-know-about-the/
39. Levin, A. 2016. '5 Reasons You Shouldn't Give Your Email Out Like Candy'. Available at: https://abcnews.go.com/Business/reasons-give-email-candy/story?id=31373966
40. Abousen, D. 'Computer Security'. Available at: http://www.contrib.andrew.cmu.edu/~dabousen/Default%20-%20Copy%20(4).html
41. *Stack Exchange*. 'What Is the context of the Quote "With Great Power Comes Great Responsibility"?' Available at: https://scifi.stackexchange.com/questions/3857/what-is-the-context-of-the-quote-with-great-power-comes-great-responsibility
42. *Michalsons Practical Legal Solutions*. 'Cybercrime Law around the World'. Available at: https://www.michalsons.com/focus-areas/internet-law-internet-regulation/cybercrime-law
43. *EnigmaSoft*. 'Top 20 Countries Found to Have the Most Cybercrime'. Available at: https://www.enigmasoftware.com/top-20-countries-the-most-cybercrime/
44. Turner, S. 2018. '2018 Data Breaches—The Worst of Last Year'. Available at: https://www.identityforce.com/blog/2018-data-breaches
45. Lord, N. 2018. 'What is Security Incident Management? The Cybersecurity Incident Management Process, Examples, Best Practices, and More'. Available at: https://digitalguardian.com/blog/what-security-incident-management-cybersecurity-incident-management-process
46. *IBM Security*. 2017. 'Ponemon Institute's 2017 Cost of Data Breach Study: Global Overview'. Available at: https://www.ibm.com/downloads/cas/ZYKLN2E3
47. *Careers in Cybersecurity*. 'Crisis Management: 7 Steps to Contain a Cyber Attack'. Available at: https://careersincybersecurity.com/crisis-management-7-steps-contain-cyber-attack/

48. *AT&T Cybersecurity Insights*. 2016. 'The CEO's Guide to Cyberbreach Response: What to Do Before, During and After a Cyberbreach'. Available at: https://www.business.att.com/content/dam/attbusiness/reports/cyberbreachresponse.pdf
49. Sheridan, K. 2018. '77% of Businesses Lack Proper Incident Response Plans'. Available at: https://www.darkreading.com/attacks-breaches/77--of-businesses-lack-proper-incident-response-plans/d/d-id/1331275
50. *Risk Control Strategies*. 2017. 'Why Don't More Companies Use Multi-factor Authentication?' Available at: https://www.riskcontrolstrategies.com/2017/11/06/dont-companies-use-multi-factor-authentication/
51. Carr, A. 'Sony PSN Hacked: A Case Study of Security Issues in Information System'. Available at: https://www.brighthub.com/computing/smb-security/articles/123382.aspx
52. Burney, S.R. 2007. 'Official Website of Maharashtra State Hacked'. Available at: http://www.arabnews.com/node/303555
53. Armerding, T. 2018. 'The 18 Biggest Data Breaches of the 21st Century'. Available at: https://www.csoonline.com/article/2130877/data-breach/the-biggest-data-breaches-of-the-21st-century.html
54. *SecureAuth*. 2017. 'Survey: Majority of Americans Reuse Passwords and Millennials are the Biggest Culprits'. Available at: https://www.secureauth.com/company/newsroom/secureauth-survey-majority-reuse-passwords
55. Lane, K., and M. McGurk. 2009. 'Leaders in the Crisis: McKinsey Global Survey Results'. Available at: https://www.mckinsey.com/business-functions/organization/our-insights/leaders-in-the-crisis-mckinsey-global-survey-results
56. *Marsh & McLennan*. 2017. '2017 Cyber Threats: A Perfect Storm about to Hit Europe?' Available at: http://www.mmc.com/content/dam/mmc-web/Files/WEF-REPORT-2017.pdf
57. Wither, D. 2016. '5 Reasons Why Small Businesses Need Cyber Security'. Available at: https://tech.co/news/should-small-businesses-be-paying-more-attention-to-cyber-security-2016-10

58. Smith, M. 2013. 'Most Costly Cybercrime Attacks: Denial-of-Service, Malicious Insider and Web-Based'. Available at: https://www.csoonline.com/article/2225534/microsoft-subnet/most-costly-cybercrime-attacks--denial-of-service--malicious-insider-and-web-based.html
59. Baig, A. 2017. '91% of Cyber Attacks Start with a Phishing Email: Here's How to Protect against Phishing'. Available at: https://digitalguardian.com/blog/91-percent-cyber-attacks-start-phishing-email-heres-how-protect-against-phishing
60. Liwer, D. 2018. '4 Main Reasons Why SMEs and SMBs Fail After a Major Cyberattack'. Available at: https://www.csoonline.com/article/3267715/cyber-attacks-espionage/4-main-reasons-why-smes-and-smbs-fail-after-a-major-cyberattack.html
61. *Cision PR Newswire.* 2018. 'IBM Study: Responding to Cybersecurity Incidents Still a Major Challenge for Businesses'. Available at: https://www.prnewswire.com/news-releases/ibm-study-responding-to-cybersecurity-incidents-still-a-major-challenge-for-businesses-300613590.html
62. Newitz, A. 2015. '9 Facts About Computer Security That Experts Wish You Knew'. Available at: https://gizmodo.com/9-facts-about-computer-security-that-experts-wish-you-k-1686817774
63. Morgan, S. 2017. 'Cybercrime Damages $6 Trillion by 2021'. Available at: https://1c7fab3im83f5gqiow2qqs2k-wpengine.netdna-ssl.com/2015-wp/wp-content/uploads/2017/10/2017-Cybercrime-Report.pdf
64. Klubnikin, A. 2017. '4 Ways IoT Changes the Financial Services Industry'. Available at: https://www.iotforall.com/4-changes-iot-in-financial-services-industry/
65. Marr, B. 2015. '17 "Internet Of Things" Facts Everyone Should Read'. Available at: https://www.forbes.com/sites/bernardmarr/2015/10/27/17-mind-blowing-internet-of-things-facts-everyone-should-read/#1526bb633505
66. *Infosys*. 2018. 'IoT-enabled Banking Services'. Available at: https://www.infosys.com/industries/financial-services/white-papers/Documents/IoT-enabled-banking.pdf

67. *Sai Industrial*. 2017. 'How Will the Internet of Things Impact the Agricultural Industry'. Available at: http://www.saiindustrial.com/how-will-the-internet-of-things-impact-the-agricultural-industry/
68. *Open Web Application Security Project*. 2014. 'Internet of Things Top Ten'. Available at: https://www.owasp.org/images/7/71/Internet_of_Things_Top_Ten_2014-OWASP.pdf
69. *Open Web Application Security Project*. 2017. 'IoT Security Guidance'. Available at: https://www.owasp.org/index.php/IoT_Security_Guidance
70. *Press Trust of India*. 2017. 'Indian Internet of Things Market Value to Touch $9 billion by 2020'. Available at: https://www.livemint.com/Industry/tF2p8P7BF39r1e1S8Xd2SJ/Indian-Internet-of-Things-market-value-to-touch-9-billion-b.html
71. Singh, I. 2017. 'India's Cybersecurity laws inadequate for IoT, Big Data, Cloud and AI'. Available at: https://www.geospatialworld.net/blogs/iot-big-data-cloud-and-cybersecurity-laws-in-india/
72. Larson, S. 2017. 'FDA Confirms that St. Jude's Cardiac Devices can be Hacked'. Available at: http://money.cnn.com/2017/01/09/technology/fda-st-jude-cardiac-hack/index.html
73. Filar, B. 2015. 'NLP For Security: Malicious Language Processing'. Available at: https://www.endgame.com/blog/technical-blog/nlp-security-malicious-language-processing
74. Lant, K. 2017. 'An Advanced AI Has Been Deployed to Fight Against Hackers'. Available at: https://futurism.com/an-advanced-ai-has-been-deployed-to-fight-against-hackers
75. Zadelhoff, M.V. 2015. 'Four Big Cyber Security Challenges (And How to Overcome Them)'. Available at: https://www.forbes.com/sites/ibm/2015/05/14/four-big-cyber-security-challenges-and-how-to-overcome-them/#7faabf585867
76. Holloway, R. 2018. 'Increasing Cyber-security with Artificial Intelligence: Learning to Predict'. Available at: https://www.scmagazineuk.com/increasing-cyber-security-artificial-intelligence-learning-predict/article/1472750

77. Dobran, B. 2018. '32 Cybersecurity Experts Predict Threats and Trends for 2018'. Available at: https://www.nationalcyberleague.org/single-post/2018/03/11/32-Cybersecurity-Experts-Predict-Threats-and-Trends-for-2018
78. Kennedy, J. 2018. 'Cybersecurity: The 'Zero-Trust' Movement. Cybersecurity Skills Shortage'. Available at: https://www.csoonline.com/article/3258994/data-protection/cybersecurity-skills-shortage.html
79. Mohanty, R. 2017. '5 Minute Guide to AI in Cyber Security'. Available at: https://www.paladion.net/blogs/5-minute-guide-to-ai-in-cyber-security
80. *Recorded Future*. 2018. 'Machine Learning: Practical Applications for Cybersecurity'. Available at: https://www.recordedfuture.com/machine-learning-cybersecurity-applications/
81. *NormShield*. 'Cyber Security with Artificial Intelligence in 10 Questions'. Available at: https://www.normshield.com/cyber-security-with-artificial-intelligence-in-10-question/
82. Ashford, W. 2017. 'Cyber Security Professionals Urged to Embrace AI and Automation'. Available at: https://www.computerweekly.com/news/450429185/Cyber-security-professionals-urged-to-embrace-AI-and-automation
83. Goldreich, O. 2004. 'The Foundations of Cryptography—Volume II'. Available at: http://www.wisdom.weizmann.ac.il/~oded/foc-vol2.html
84. Abadi, M., and D.G. Andersen. 2016. 'Learning to Protect Communications with Adversarial Neural Cryptography'. Available at: https://arxiv.org/pdf/1610.06918v1.pdf
85. *Cisco*. 2018. 'Cisco 2018 Annual Cybersecurity Report Reveals Security Leaders Rely on and Invest in Automation, Machine Learning and Artificial Intelligence to Defend Against Threats'. Available at:https://investor.cisco.com/investor-relations/news-and-events/news/news-details/2018/Cisco-2018-Annual-Cybersecurity-Report-Reveals-Security-Leaders-Rely-on-and-Invest-in-Automation-Machine-Learning-and-Artificial-Intelligence-to-Defend-Against-Threats/default.aspx

86. Mina, G. 2017. 'AI is the Future of Cybersecurity – How Watson Helps Detect Threats Faster and Better Protect Your Organization'. Available at: https://www.ibm.com/blogs/watson/2017/08/ai-is-the-future-of-cybersecurity-how-watson-helps-detect-threats-faster-and-better-protect-your-organization/
87. Abramsky, J. 2017. 'The Future of Cyber Security: One Small Step for Man, One Giant Leap for AI'. Available at: https://medium.com/qtma-insights/the-future-of-cyber-security-one-small-step-for-man-one-giant-leap-for-ai-5133a2ab335a
88. Ashford, W. 2017. 'McAfee Forges Ahead with Analytics, Deep Learning and AI'. Available at: https://www.computerweekly.com/news/450428465/McAfee-forges-ahead-with-analytics-deep-learning-and-AI
89. *Darktrace*. 'The Enterprise Immune System: Detects and Fights Cyber-threats in Real Time'. Available at: https://www.darktrace.com/technology/
90. *Cylance*. 2017. 'The Artificial Intelligence Revolution in Cybersecurity: How Prevention Achieves Superior ROI and Efficacy'. Available at: https://pages.cylance.com/rs/524-DOM-989/images/AI_eBook.pdf?utm_medium=Blog
91. Hern, A. 2018. 'Growth of AI Could Boost Cybercrime and Security Threats, Report Warns'. Available at: https://www.theguardian.com/technology/2018/feb/21/ai-security-threats-cybercrime-political-disruption-physical-attacks-report
92. Jackson, K.L. 2011. 'Cloud to Command 90% of Microsoft's R&D Budget'. Available at: https://www.forbes.com/sites/kevinjackson/2011/04/19/cloud-to-command-90-of-microsofts-rd-budget/#7ada384d571b
93. Bourne, J. 2017. 'British Medical Journal expands to China with help of Alibaba Cloud and Datapipe'. Available at: https://www.cloudcomputing-news.net/news/2017/sep/07/british-medical-journal-expands-china-help-alibaba-cloud-and-datapipe/

94. Frankenfield, J. 2019. 'Cloud Computing'. Available at: https://www.investopedia.com/terms/c/cloud-computing.asp
95. *Business Wire India*. 2017. 'Salesforce Releases New Research on the Salesforce Economy—Creating 3.3 Million New Jobs and $859 Billion in New Business Revenues Worldwide By 2022'. Available at: https://www.thehindubusinessline.com/business-wire/salesforce-releases-new-research-on-the-salesforce-economy-creating-33-million-new-jobs-and-859-billion-in-new-business-revenues-worldwide-by-2022/article9925850.ece
96. *Microsoft Azure*. 'What is Cloud Computing?' Available at: https://azure.microsoft.com/en-in/overview/what-is-cloud-computing/
97. *Microsoft Azure*. 'What is SaaS?' Available at: https://azure.microsoft.com/en-in/overview/what-is-saas/
98. Rouse, M., and S. Bigelow. 2017. 'Platform as a Service (PaaS)'. Available at: https://searchcloudcomputing.techtarget.com/definition/Platform-as-a-Service-PaaS
99. *Arcitura*. 'Cloud Deployment Models'. Available at: http://whatiscloud.com/cloud_deployment_models/public_clouds
100. Mahale, S. 2018. 'How Cloud Computing Can Empower India's Vision of a "Digital-First" Country'. Available at: https://inc42.com/resources/cloud-computing-digital-first-country/
101. *Press Trust of India*. 2018. 'Over 53,000 Cyber Security Incidents observed in 2017'. Available at: https://www.thehindubusinessline.com/info-tech/over-53000-cyber-security-incidents-observed-in-2017/article22705876.ece
102. *Press Trust of India*. 2018. 'India Ranks 3rd Among Nations Facing Most Cyber Threats: Symantec'. Available at: https://economictimes.indiatimes.com/tech/internet/india-ranks-3rd-among-nations-facing-most-cyber-threats-symantec/articleshow/63616106.cms
103. *Economic Times Bureau*. 2017. 'India Third Worst Hit Nation by Ransomware Wannacry; Over 40,000

Computers Affected'. Available at: https://economictimes.indiatimes.com/tech/internet/india-third-worst-hit-nation-by-ransomware-wannacry-over-40000-computers-affected/articleshow/58707260.cms

104. *Press Trust of India*. 2017. 'Petya Ransomware Cyberattack: India Worst Hit in Asia Pacific Region, Claims Symantec'. Available at: https://indianexpress.com/article/technology/tech-news-technology/india-worst-hit-by-petya-in-apac-7th-globally-symantec-4727656/

105. Ajgaonkar, P. 2017. '94pc of Cyber Attacks are Caused by Lack of Infosecurity Awareness. Is Your Organization Safe?' Available at: https://yourstory.com/2017/11/94pc-cyber-attacks-caused-lack-infosecurity-awareness/

106. *Press Trust of India*. 2018. 'Over 53000 Cyber-Security Incidents Observed in 2017'. Available at: https://www.thehindubusinessline.com/info-tech/over-53000-cyber-security-incidents-observed-in-2017/article22705876.ece

107. Tech Desk. 2017. 'Locky Ransomware Hits Indian Cyberspace, Government Issues Alert'. Available at: https://indianexpress.com/article/technology/tech-news-technology/locky-ransomware-hits-indian-cyberspace-government-issues-alert/

108. Mukul, P. 2016. 'Cyber Security: NSA-administered Rs 1,000-cr Fund Kept Open to Private Players'. Available at: https://indianexpress.com/article/india/india-news-india/cyber-security-nsa-administered-rs-1000-cr-fund-kept-open-to-private-players-3740699/

109. Srivastava, M. 2016. 'India Eyes Indigenous Expertise in Cyber-security, to Fund Security Start-ups'. Available at: https://www.business-standard.com/article/economy-policy/india-eyes-ind.igenous-expertise-in-cyber-security-to-fund-security-start-ups-116100900419_1.html

110. *SSC NASSCOM*. 2015. 'NASSCOM Partners with Symantec for Building Cyber Security Skills in India'. Available at: http://www.sscnasscom.com/building-cyber-secutrity-skills/

111. Weston, P. 2018. 'The 25 Worst Passwords of 2018: Cybersecurity Firm Reveals Top Offenders When it Comes to Leaving Yourself Open to Hackers (and 123456 is Number One!)' Available at: https://www.dailymail.co.uk/sciencetech/article-6496125/The-25-worst-passwords-2018-Cybersecurity-firm-reveals-offenders.html
112. *IANS*. 2019. 'Indane Leaked Millions of Aadhaar Numbers: French Security Researcher'. Available at: https://economictimes.indiatimes.com/news/politics-and-nation/indane-leaked-millions-of-aadhaar-numbers-french-security-researcher/articleshow/68058639.cms
113. Huang, S. 'Cyber Criminals' Exploitation of Artificial Intelligence'. Available at: https://www.nscs.gov.sg/irahss-2017-think-pieces/public-data/doc/cyber-criminals-exploitation-of-artificial-intelligence-by-sochenda-huang.pdf
114. Meulen, N.V.D. 2013. 'DigiNotar: Dissecting the First Dutch Digital Disaster'. Available at: http://dx.doi.org/10.5038/1944-0472.6.2.4

ABOUT THE AUTHORS

Rodney D. Ryder is a partner with Scriboard, a full-service commercial law firm with cutting edge specialisation in technology, new media and intellectual property laws. He is presently advisor to the Ministry of Communications and Information Technology, Government of India, on the implementation of the Information Technology Act, 2000. Ryder is also advisor to the Data Security Council of India, an initiative of the National Association of Software and Services Companies (NASSCOM) on the structuring of industry data privacy and information-security policies, and contractual standards.

Ryder has been nominated as a 'leading lawyer' in intellectual property, technology, communications and media law by *asialaw*, *Who's Who Legal*, *The Legal 500 Asia Pacific* amongst other international publications. He is the author of *Guide to Cyber Laws (Information Technology Act, 2000e-Commerce, Data Protection and The Internet)*, the first section-wise analysis of the Indian Information Technology Act, 2000. His second book, *Intellectual Property and the Internet*, published by LexisNexis, is perhaps the only one of its kind in Asia. The text has been acknowledged to be a work of authority by the Hon'ble Supreme Court of India and has been quoted in the first and only judgement by the Hon'ble Supreme Court of India on domain names (Satyam Infoway Ltd vs Sifynet Solutions Pvt. Ltd, 2004, 6 SCC 145). He is advisor to the National Internet Exchange of India (NiXI) and a member of the panel of independent and neutral arbitrators with NiXI.

Ashwin Madhavan is the co-founder and CEO of Enhelion, an online legal management education company, focused on bridging the gap between the academia and the corporate world. He has successfully managed to bootstrap Enhelion since its inception in 2013. Madhavan completed his graduation in law from Gujarat National Law University (GNLU) and holds a master's degree from Dalhousie University, Canada. He worked in Canada for a while before returning to India. His areas of expertise are domain names and cybersquatting, trademarks, copyrights and information-technology laws. He was a member of the Canadian Bar Association and has advised numerous Fortune 500 companies on various aspects of India's technology and IP Laws.

Madhavan has authored three books and is the editor of five books. His first book, published in 2014, has been translated into Mandarin for readers of the People's Republic of China. Ashwin loves to read books related to history, business management and foreign policy. Travelling the world is his passion and he often takes out time to travel to new places.